Will I Get Breast Cancer?

Questions & Answers for Teenage Girls

D1509184

by Carole Garbuny Vogel

Julian Messner
Published by Silver Burdett Press
Morristown, New Jersey

The goal of this book is to provide general information about breast cancer and related issues. It is not intended to substitute for the advice of a physician or other health-care professional.

Copyright © 1995 by Carole Garbuny Vogel

Illustrations by Joel Ito
Designed by Sylvia Frezzolini Severance, with Rosemary Buonocore
Graphs on pages 55 and 56 by Erik S. MacPeek

Published by Julian Messner, a division of Silver Burdett Press, Morristown, NJ 07960.
Julian Messner and colophon are trademarks of Simon & Schuster

10 9 8 7 6 5 4 3 2 1

Library of Congress Cataloging-in-Publication Data

Vogel, Carole Garbuny.
    Will I get breast cancer? : questions & answers for teenage girls
  by Carole Garbuny Vogel.
    p. cm.
    Includes bibliographical references and index.
    1. Breast—Cancer—Juvenile literature. [1. Breast—Cancer.
  2. Cancer. 3. Diseases. 4. Questions and answers.] I. Title.
  RC280.B8V64 1995   94-21979
  616.99' 449—dc20   CIP
                                                  AC
  ISBN 0-671-88046-2 (hardcover)
  ISBN 0-671-88047-0 (paperback)

For Hilary Ann Barshay
in memory of her mother
Sharon Luftglas Barshay
(1955–1987)
"Her glow has warmed the world."

Contents

Preface

It is frightening to learn that someone you know or love has breast cancer. Most of us have mental pictures of what it is like to have cancer and what it is like to undergo cancer treatments. We construct these images from rumors we hear and from "facts" we glean from television, newspapers, and magazines. Unfortunately, these sources of information are often misleading and paint a very gloomy and depressing picture of what breast cancer is like. It's hard *not* to be scared by all this.

There is a way to deal with the fear, and that is with the truth. The things we imagine about breast cancer are often far worse than what is true about breast cancer. Knowledge gives you power over fear.

Some of the facts about breast cancer should be stated right now and remembered again and again:

- First, most women who get breast cancer *do not* die of breast cancer.
- Second, most girls whose mothers had breast cancer *do not* develop breast cancer themselves.
- Third, treatments for breast cancer are improving all the time.
- And finally, some of the smartest people in the world are doing research right now on early detection and even prevention of breast cancer. Maybe your generation will not have to worry about breast cancer the same way your mother's generation has had to.

As you read this book, you will learn other important facts that will help you understand breast cancer and its treatments. If your mother or someone else in your life has cancer, this book will make you better able to help her and the rest of your family during these difficult times. It will probably make you feel better, too. Remember, you *can* beat your fears!

Barbara L. Smith, M.D., Ph.D., Director
Massachusetts General Hospital
Comprehensive Breast Health Center

Acknowledgments

I would like to thank a number of people for their assistance in making this book a reality.

I am indebted to Barbara Smith, M.D., Ph.D., F.A.C.S., Director, Comprehensive Breast Health Center, Massachusetts General Hospital in Boston, who took time from her busy schedule to read and critique the manuscript. Her keen intellect and compassion for her patients were reflected in her comments.

I am grateful to the following mental health professionals for their time and insight: Dr. Robert S. Delulio, licensed counseling psychologist, Wellesley Hills, Massachusetts; my sister Ellen V. Garbuny, L.S.W., Butler, Pennsylvania; and Rosalie Gerut, M.A., Milton, Massachusetts.

A special thanks goes to Joyce A. Nettleton, D.Sc., R.D., Director, Science Communications at the Institute of Food Technologists in Chicago, for her invaluable criticisms and scientific expertise.

I am also grateful to Elaine Blume and Tom Reynolds of the Office of Cancer Communications at the National Cancer Institute in Bethesda, Maryland, for providing data and answering questions; my sister, Vivian Prunier, Ph.D. of the Office of Pesticide Programs, Environmental Protection Agency in Washington, D.C., for contributing up-to-date information on environmental contaminants; Don Backner, Director of Imaging Services, MetroWest Medical Center in Framingham, Massachusetts, for sharing his expertise; Karen Funkenstein, a science teacher at the Winsor School in Boston, for her insight into instructing preteen and teenage girls; Karen Petersen for sharing her personal experiences; the American Cancer Society in Waltham, Massachusetts, for supplying information; the librarians at Cary Memorial Library in Lexington, Massachusetts, for their patience and help in tracking down the most obscure facts; my former high school biology teacher, Joan Gottlieb, Ph.D. of Pittsburgh, for reviewing the manuscript; and my agents, Reneé Cho and Dorothy Markinko of McIntosh and Otis, Inc., who had the wisdom to match me with my discerning editor, Adriane Ruggiero.

I am indebted to fellow writers Florence Harris, Susan Sekuler, and Barbara Ehrlich White for their advice and support. I am especially grateful for the input from my preteen and teenage critics, Hilary Barshay, Katy Vogel, Rachel Prunier, and Sarah Prunier for reading the manuscript and telling me what worked and what didn't.

I would like to acknowledge the help of many other people who helped either directly or indirectly. Where the opinions of experts conflicted, I used my own judgment in presenting the information.

I would like to thank my husband, Mark A. Vogel, for his encouragement and understanding, especially when dinners became his responsibility. I am grateful to my children, Joshua and Katy, for understanding that "I'll be done in a minute," really meant, "I need another hour. Go fend for yourselves." Without the support of my family this book would have been impossible to write.

Dear Reader,

Seven years ago my closest friend, Sharon Luftglas Barshay, died of breast cancer. She was only 32 and she left behind her husband, a six-year-old daughter, a four-year-old son, her parents, two sisters, a huge extended family, many friends, and me.

Sharon was a pediatric nurse. She loved children, dancing, music, traditions, and most of all, her family and friends. I miss her wisdom, her compassion, and her laughter. And I miss the person I was in her presence. I loved being her friend.

What makes me the most angry about Sharon's death is that it was probably preventable. Sharon's own grandmother had died of breast cancer and Sharon knew that she might develop the disease when she was older. She examined her breasts regularly and one day discovered a small lump. At the time she was a nursing mother and she thought the lump was related to breast milk production. She waited until the baby was weaned before checking it out with her doctor.

Her doctor dismissed her concerns. He said he didn't think the lump was cancerous. But the lump continued to grow and three months later, Sharon consulted a different doctor. Within days the diagnosis of breast cancer was made and my friend's three-year battle with cancer commenced.

She never had a fighting chance. By the time treatment had begun, the cancer had already spread to distant parts of her body. If her cancer had been detected at an early stage, Sharon would probably be alive today.

At her funeral, I vowed that Sharon's death would make a difference. This book is a fulfillment of that promise. As I was writing it I often wondered what Sharon would think. I finally decided her reaction would be, *Are you crazy? This book is going to scare kids to death!* And she would be almost right.

Breast cancer is a very scary subject and as much as I have tried, I couldn't tell you what you need to know without writing a lot of upsetting stuff. I wish I could be with you to help you through the difficult parts of this book. Since I can't, you might find it helpful to discuss the worrisome parts with a parent, your doctor or nurse, or another adult who you trust.

I have tried to anticipate your questions and your concerns about breast cancer. For easy reading, the information appears in a question and answer format. It ranges from the highly technical to the very emotional. You can skip over the questions that don't interest you and concentrate on the ones that do. Or you can read the book from beginning to end to get the big picture. You can even pass over some chapters near the beginning of the book and go back to them later. Do what best meets your needs.

The most important chapters are Chapters Four and Six. Chapter Four tells you what you can do to protect yourself from breast cancer. It also explains how you can detect the disease early when the cancer can most easily be cured. This chapter is MUST reading even if you skip the rest of the book. Chapter Six talks about feelings and what to expect if your mother (or someone else close to you) is undergoing cancer treatment. As for the other chapters:

- Chapter One answers questions you may have about breasts and about your own changing body.
- Chapter Two describes the nature of cancer.
- Chapter Three discusses *risk*—the likelihood of getting breast cancer.
- Chapter Five explains how breast cancer is diagnosed and treated.
- Chapter Seven offers help if someone close to you is losing the battle to cancer.
- Chapter Eight forecasts advances in research that may make cancer easier to prevent and cure in the future.

Take charge of your health! You have an excellent chance of living to a ripe old age even with a family history of breast cancer. I hope you will find this book helpful.

Sincerely,

Carole G. Vogel

Chapter One:
Breast Basics

If you are between ten and seventeen, big changes are taking place in your body. You are changing from a young girl into a young woman. Your hips are getting wider, your breasts are developing. If it hasn't happened already, pubic hair will soon appear, your periods will start, and you will have the body of a teenager.

With a teenage body comes teenage concerns and lots of questions. *What is happening to me? Am I normal? Why am I getting pimples? Will I ever fall in love?* You probably have one big additional concern if your mother, grandmother, aunt, or sister had breast cancer, namely—*Will I get breast cancer, too?*

This chapter describes the changes taking place in your body and answers basic questions about breast cancer. Other chapters give more in-depth information on cancer, its diagnosis, and its treatment. You need to take responsibility for your own health and breast care. The information in this book will help you be more responsible.

Why are my breasts growing?

Your body changes during puberty so you can become a mother someday and produce milk, the baby's first food. One of the most noticeable changes occurs in your breasts. On the outside, they grow bigger and the nipples begin to darken and stick out. On the inside, changes take place to allow the breasts to make and store milk.

Breasts, like people, come in different shapes and sizes: big or small, pointy or flat, high or low, firm or droopy. The small tip of the breast is called the *nipple*. The nipple is where the milk will come out if you have a baby. The *areola*, a circle of darker skin, surrounds the nipple.

What is inside my breasts?

Each of your breasts contains 15 to 20 *milk glands* arranged like spokes in a wheel. Fat fills the spaces surrounding them. A milk gland looks like a tiny bunch of grapes. It branches into small clusters called *lobules* where milk can be produced. Every milk gland has its own set of *ducts* or tubes that lead to the nipple. If you become a nursing mother, milk will travel through the ducts to the outside of your nipples. Breasts also consist of nerves, blood vessels, lymph vessels, and connective tissue. No muscles are found in breasts but muscles lie beneath them in the chest.

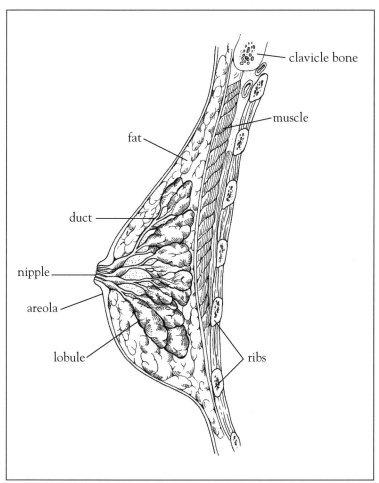

Cross section of the breast

When does breast development begin?

Girls usually begin to develop breasts when they are about 10 or 11 years old. Some girls develop earlier and some girls develop later. Many girls worry that they are maturing either too early or too late. You need not worry! Everyone's rate of development is different.

The starting age of development will not affect the ultimate size of your breasts when you finish maturing. Early starters can end up with big breasts or small, and it is the same for late starters—they can wind up with big or small breasts. In addition, your starting age has nothing to do with how fast your breasts will develop. Early starters can grow quickly or slowly. Likewise, the breasts of late starters can grow fast or slow.

Wouldn't it be much simpler if every girl began to develop breasts on the day she entered seventh grade and everybody finished up a year later with the same size breasts? Then no girl would worry about whether she was normal or not! But that's not the way it is. Breasts differ from individual to individual just as noses, eyes, and feet do.

No matter when you start, your breast development goes through several stages. During childhood, breasts are flat with a slightly-raised nipple. When the breasts begin to develop, the nipple and areola darken and enlarge. Small buds of breast tissue grow beneath the nipple and areola, pushing them out. These buds contain milk ducts and fat. During development they can feel itchy or uncomfortable. Even though your breasts may look or feel as if they are going to burst, don't worry, they won't!

In the next stage, the breast itself becomes large and protrudes more from the chest. The nipple and areola continue to darken and grow. Then the breasts continue to enlarge. The nipple and areola may form separate bulges and stick out from the breasts, but some girls skip this stage. In the final stage, the breasts become rounder and fuller. The aerola sinks back into the contour of the breast.

Lots of girls are excited and proud of their blossoming breasts. Others are embarrassed by the changes in their body and feel more comfortable wearing bulky sweaters and oversized shirts to hide their breasts. When these girls grow older and more secure with their figures, they may switch to more form-fitting clothing.

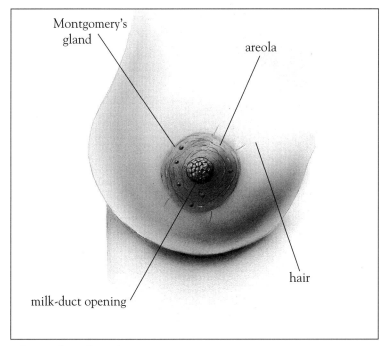

The nipple and areola

Will exercise make my breasts bigger?

No! Chest exercises will strengthen the muscles *beneath* the breasts but cannot increase bust size. Your breasts consist mainly of glandular tissue and fat. Most of their roundness comes from the fat. If you are underweight and small-breasted, your breasts *may* become fuller if you gain weight, but heredity plays the major role in determining breast size. Some girls who consider themselves to be flat-chested may still be in the process of developing.

What do breasts have to do with sex?

Ever since you were an infant, you have known that your body can give you pleasurable feelings. It is natural to want to show affection for other people through closeness and touch. Babies and young children need lots of cuddling and physical contact with their parents. You may have gotten lots of hugs and kisses while you were growing up. When you are ready for a loving relationship with a partner, you will discover that kissing and touching can stir strong feelings of warmth and pleasure.

While expressing their love to their partners, many women enjoy having their breasts stroked and kissed. This kind of touching can make a woman ready for sexual intercourse. Some women enjoy having their breasts sucked, too. This behavior is natural and will not lead to cancer. Other women find breast stimulation unexciting or unpleasant. Nothing is wrong with them—they just respond to different stimulation.

Small or big breasts—what's the fuss?

Big or little, the size of your breasts has nothing to do with your sexuality or your ability to nurse a baby. Small breasts can give the same pleasurable feeling as big breasts when they are caressed. Small breasts can produce just as much milk as big ones.

Yet you live in a society that makes a big fuss about big busts. TV shows, movies, and advertisements with beautiful, large-breasted women bombard you with the idea that bigger is better. Because of all this hype, some women with small breasts may feel unattractive. They feel they can't be alluring or desirable. For these women, padded bras, and bra inserts called "falsies" may help them feel more attractive.

Padded bras contain a thick layer of cotton, synthetic fiber, or foam rubber in the cups. Bra inserts are breast-shaped molds that fit inside bra cups. They are kind of like shoulder pads for the chest. Padded bras and bra inserts give the appearance of having a larger bust.

Big breasts can cause distress, too. A girl with a large bust may be teased by her classmates and receive unwelcome stares and comments when she is out in public. In overweight girls, a sensible weight loss *may* reduce the size of the breasts. Special bras called "minimizers" can help too. They make the breasts appear less prominent.

If you dread gym class, you are not alone. Many, many girls hate undressing in front of their classmates, and even worse, taking group showers afterward. Some girls are modest and feel uncomfortable removing their clothes in public. Others are ashamed of their bodies. If you find the locker-room routine totally humiliating, remember, there are probably lots of other girls with you who are just as self-conscious about themselves or even more so.

Do you need big breasts to be feminine?

Some people link femininity to big breasts. Being feminine, however, has little to do with breasts. It is a state of mind. Being feminine means being secure about the physical and emotional aspects of yourself that make you female. It also means accepting yourself for who you are. You can express your femininity through clothing, speech, mannerisms, and actions. No one can take away your femininity and make you feel that you are less of a girl or a woman unless you let them. With maturity, you can learn to overcome any feelings of inadequacy by accepting and appreciating your own body. You are unique!

Can extremely big breasts be a health problem?

For some people, extremely big breasts may trigger severe backaches, breathing difficulties, and posture problems. The sheer weight of the breasts can cause bra straps to cut into the shoulders. Some women with huge breasts choose breast-reduction surgery to make their breasts smaller. Most surgeons will not perform this surgery on a young woman until she has finished developing totally.

Do women with big breasts have a greater chance of getting breast cancer?

No! Breast size has no connection to breast cancer.

Is something wrong if one breast is bigger than the other?

Most women have slightly unequal breasts, just as they have slightly unequal feet. The difference is barely visible.

However, in many people, one breast may be noticeably larger than the other. If you are lopsided, don't worry about it! The problem may correct itself within a year or two since breasts grow at different rates.

What are stretch marks?

Stretch marks are reddish streaks that can appear on the skin when you gain or lose weight quickly. They occur when the elastic fibers of the skin lose their resilience. Some girls develop them on their breasts during rapid breast growth. Although they are permanent, stretch marks may lighten and become less visible. They are harmless.

Is it normal to have hair grow around the nipple?

Lots of women grow hair around their nipples. If nipple hair bothers you, you can shave it, pluck it, or even use electrolysis to get rid of it. Pulling out nipple hair will not cause cancer.

Why does the shape of the nipple and areola change?

The nipples and areolas may lie almost flat in a relaxed state. But they may pucker up and stiffen when you are cold, during sexual stimulation, when they rub against clothing, and in breast feeding. This stiffening occurs when tiny muscle fibers in the areola contract.

What are inverted nipples?

Nipples that pucker inward instead of sticking outward are called inverted nipples. They are caused by tissue inside the breast that holds the nipple down. This condition is usually present at birth but may not be noticeable until later. It can occur in one or both breasts. Nursing with inverted nipples may be difficult, but sometimes inverted nipples turn outward during breast development or pregnancy. A normal nipple that suddenly becomes inverted later in life (or an inverted nipple that suddenly sticks out) may signal the growth of an underlying tumor, and should be checked by a doctor or nurse.

An inverted nipple

Should I worry about a discharge from my nipple?

Most women secrete a small amount of fluid through their nipples. Usually so little fluid is produced that the discharge isn't noticeable. Some girls and women, however, can produce a visible discharge when they squeeze their nipples. The fluid may come in a variety of colors—white, gray, green, or yellow. Women who take birth control pills may find that their discharge increases.

Most nipple discharge in teenagers is absolutely normal. However, in *rare* cases it can indicate a problem. Infections can create a discharge with pus. Warty growths in the lining of a milk duct can cause a bloody discharge. So can pregnancy. Precancerous growths (abnormal-looking cells), and even more rarely, cancer itself can cause an unusual discharge. *Most likely any discharge you have will be normal.* However, if you have any questions, do not hesitate to discuss them with your nurse or physician.

Do I have to wear a bra?

Wearing a bra is a personal decision that is entirely up to you. There is no medical reason to wear one although there may be social pressure to use one or avoid one. Many girls and women with small or firm breasts may not bother with bras. If you are large-breasted or if you engage in athletic activities, you may find it more comfortable to wear one. Bras with an underwire sewn in the base of the cups provide extra support. Athletic bras hold the breasts close to the chest to keep them from jiggling. Bras will not prevent sagging as you age.

Why do some people use slang words to refer to breasts?

Sometimes talking about breasts can be uncomfortable. Using the proper scientific name makes some people nervous because the word can carry strong emotional feelings. They may be embarrassed to say the word breast, or they may think it is a "dirty" word. Others may consider the breasts so private they should not be talked about.

Some of the slang words for breasts are *boobs, jugs, tits,* knockers, headlights, honkers, hooters, milkers, bosooms, and melons. These words are often used by boys and men in a joking way but they can be hurtful, especially if used in an offensive way. Many women refer to their breasts with less highly charged words such as bust, chest, or bosom.

What can I do about boys who make comments about my breasts?

Many girls feel embarrassed or humiliated when boys stare or make comments about their breasts. In our culture, many boys and men think nothing of taunting females. Often they find it amusing to use offensive slang in referring to a woman's breast. Sadly, almost every woman and teenage girl in our society will experience some kind of verbal harassment about her anatomy.

Some girls feel flattered when boys or men whistle or make comments about their bodies. Many others find the attention demeaning and often frightening, especially when groups of boys or men yell out as they walk by.

It is dangerous for you to confront a stranger who harasses you, but you can try to make changes in your school. Perhaps you and your friends can ask a sympathetic teacher, principal, or guidance counselor to deal with problem boys and address the issue of harassment on a school-wide basis or in health or life-skills classes. Try not to take this kind of harassment to heart. It is an act of hostility that shows contempt and lack of respect for all girls and women, not necessarily for you personally. By taking group action, you may be able to change the environment in your school or where you work.

What is a period?

You were born with two *ovaries*, small organs in the abdomen that contain thousands of undeveloped egg cells. The ovaries are not active until puberty begins and the eggs start to develop. This usually occurs between the ages of 9 and 15—sometimes earlier, sometimes later. Each month, one or the other ovary produces and releases a mature egg. The egg travels down the Fallopian tubes toward the uterus. If it is fertilized by a sperm from a man, the fertilized egg will attach itself to the uterus and develop into a baby. Most of the time, the egg doesn't meet with a sperm and it simply breaks apart.

During the days before the egg's release, the uterus prepares for a fertilized egg. It creates a nourishing, blood-filled lining, the perfect environment for a developing baby to grow. If the egg isn't fertilized, the blood-filled lining is not needed. The body discards the lining along with the unfertilized egg. The blood passes through the vagina and out of the body. This discharge is called *menstruation* and lasts a few days to a week. Many women refer to it as "having their period." After it stops, the uterus builds up a new lining and a new egg is released. The entire cycle takes about a month. If that egg is not fertilized, the new lining will break down and another period will occur.

The first period is called *menarche*. It may take more

than a year or two for periods to become regular. The menstrual cycle repeats itself for many years but does not last forever. Some time between the ages of 45 and 55 women go through a process called *menopause* or "change of life." They stop producing eggs and having periods.

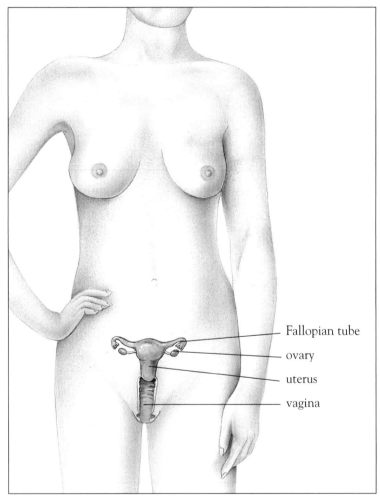

Fallopian tube

ovary

uterus

vagina

The internal female sexual organs

What are hormones and what part do they play?

Each stage in your menstrual cycle is controlled by *hormones*—special chemicals made by glands. The subject of hormones is *very* complicated—your body makes many different kinds, including the two main female sex hormones *estrogen* and *progesterone*. These two hormones are manufactured in the ovaries and released into the bloodstream. Then they travel to other parts of the body.

Progesterone readies the uterus to receive the fertilized egg. It also helps prepare the breasts to make milk. Estrogen causes many of the changes you see as you develop into a woman, including the growth of breasts, the appearance of underarm and pubic hair, and the rounding of your hips, thighs, and buttocks.

Why do my breasts change each month before I get my period?

Hormonal changes during the week before your period may cause a little swelling and tenderness in your breasts. They may also cause other physical changes such as pimples, a bloated feeling, or temporary weight gain, and they may also affect your mood. Some girls become irritable or depressed. These physical and emotional changes are referred to as *PMS*—or *premenstrual syndrome*. Even before you get your period for the first time, you may experience hormonal changes and mood swings.

Will my breasts change during pregnancy?

Your breasts will begin to change soon after you

become pregnant. For some women, sore breasts or nipples may be the first sign that they are pregnant. Your breasts will grow bigger and become firmer. The areola will darken and the nipples will become larger and more erect. After the baby is born, your breasts will begin to produce milk. This takes about three to five days. In the meantime, your breasts will make *colostrum*, a liquid filled with antibodies to help the baby fight infections.

What happens to breasts when a baby nurses?

When a baby nurses, it sucks some milk out of the breast into its mouth. This sucking stimulates the breast to speed the flow of milk to the nipple. The mother experiences a tingling sensation and the milk flows out. Sucking also sends a message to the mother's body to make more milk. So the more the baby nurses, the more milk the breasts produce.

When the baby moves on to solid foods and gradually stops nursing, the mother's milk supply will diminish and eventually disappear. This process is called *weaning*.

Why do I worry about my breasts?

Many girls feel that the changes in their bodies signal an unwelcome change in their lives. They are unsure about leaving their childhood. They are worried about growing up and taking on all the responsibilities adulthood involves. The maturing process doesn't happen overnight. You have all of your adolescent years to adjust to your

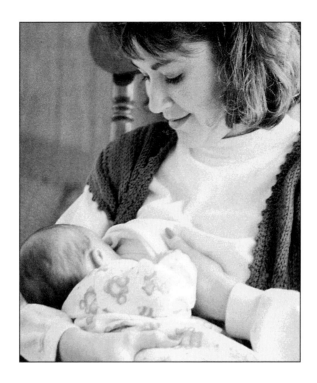

changing body and your emerging adulthood. Adolescence has many ups and downs.

When your body first started to develop breasts, you realized that you were becoming a woman like your mother. All girls think they will be like their mothers in some ways when they grow up. This can be scary to think about if your mother had breast cancer.

Many girls with a family history of breast cancer fear their own breasts. When they touch their chests, every bone, every bump feels like a lump of cancer. These girls may connect becoming a woman with losing a breast, or becoming ill and dying of cancer. Breast cancer is extremely rare before the age of 25, so it is very unlikely that you will get breast cancer as a teenager. Don't let yourself worry! Talk to your nurse or doctor if anything about your breasts concerns you. Unusual breast lumps should be evaluated in women of any age.

Should I worry about breast pain?

Sometimes one or both of your breasts may feel tender or sore. This is a normal part of becoming a woman. Slight swelling and tenderness in your breast may be caused by hormonal changes during the week before your period. If you keep track of your periods on a calendar, you can tell if these hormonal changes are the cause of your breast pain. Simply count three weeks past the beginning of your last period.

Some teenage girls (and boys) develop a painful "adolescent nodule" beneath the nipple. These lumps are harmless and usually disappear in a short time. (Cancerous lumps are usually not painful.)

Sore, lumpy breasts can create needless alarm although the vast majority of lumps are harmless. Some lumps come and go depending on the stage of the menstrual cycle. However, they can be a very scary experience if you are worried about breast cancer. To put your mind at ease about any unusual lumps, you may want to ask your nurse or doctor about it.

If my mother had breast cancer, will I get it, too?

This is probably one of the scariest questions you will

ever ask, but you are not alone. Every daughter of a breast-cancer patient worries about the same thing. The answer is scary, too. If your mother had breast cancer, then you have a slightly greater chance of getting it when you reach adulthood then the average woman.

Behind your question *Will I get breast cancer?* is another: **If I get breast cancer will I die from it?** Early breast cancer can be cured, but the outlook becomes less favorable when the cancer is quite advanced. Women have an excellent chance of beating breast cancer if they take charge of their health. As you read this book, you will learn about the many things you can do to reduce your risk of dying from breast cancer. Breast-cancer prevention and detection are discussed in Chapter Four.

Chapter Two:
What *Is* Cancer, Anyway?

The word *cancer* is a frightening word, especially if someone you love has cancer. It is even more scary if you think you will get it, too. This chapter will help you understand what cancer is. Perhaps, when you finish reading, you will find cancer a little less menacing. However, if you find this chapter too technical you can skip it for now and go onto another one. You can always come back to it later.

What does cancer have to do with cells?

Cancer is a disease of the cells. To grasp the mystery of cancer you need to understand how healthy cells work. You probably already know that cells are the smallest living part of your body. They come in many different shapes and sizes—some are round, some are flat. Others look like long, thin threads or buttons without holes. Most cells are too small to see without the aid of a microscope.

Your cells are bubble-like sacs containing tiny parts called *organelles*, and large molecules. A thin *cell membrane* surrounds each cell, protecting it and separating it from neighboring cells. An internal communications network enables the cell to sense and respond to change in its environment and to interact with other cells.

How do cells get what they need?

Blood provides everything the cell needs—food, water, and oxygen. To enter, these materials must pass through the cell membrane. Carbon dioxide and other wastes pass through the cell membrane to exit. The bloodstream then carries them away.

What do cells do?

Each kind of cell has a specific job. Skin cells cover and protect the body, nerve cells carry messages, and red blood cells transport oxygen. If you have a baby, the specialized cells in your breasts' glands will produce milk.

Cells that grow and work together form a *tissue*. In most tissues a kind of "cement" fills the spaces between cells. It binds cells to one another in the way mortar holds bricks together. Different kinds of tissue join together to form an *organ*. Your breasts are glandular organs designed to make milk.

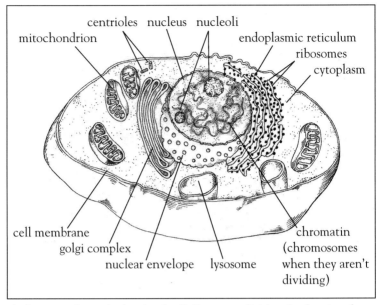

centrioles   nucleus   nucleoli
mitochondrion
endoplasmic reticulum
ribosomes
cytoplasm
cell membrane
golgi complex
nuclear envelope   lysosome
chromatin
(chromosomes
when they aren't
dividing)

A diagram of a typical animal cell (between divisions), showing the major parts

How are cells controlled?

Deep inside the cell lies its control center—the *nucleus*. Its power lies in its ability to permit the cell to reproduce. All true cells contain a nucleus. *Chromosomes*, the threadlike structures within the nucleus, direct all the cell's activities, including growth and reproduction. In a process called *cell division*, a full-grown cell divides into two new ones.

You make new cells all the time. You need them to grow and to replace damaged and worn out cells. In some parts of your body such as your skin, cell division occurs more frequently than in others.

Cells cannot live forever—they age and die—but the

cells in your body vary in life span. Your red blood cells live about 120 days and are continually being replaced. Your nerve cells can last your entire lifetime.

What happens during cell division?

During cell division many changes take place in the nucleus. The chromosomes make exact copies of themselves and separate. One nucleus becomes two and the cell begins to pull apart. New cell membranes form when the old cell membrane breaks apart. Two identical cells now exist where once there was one. Each new cell is complete and can contribute to the health of your body. If more cells are needed, the cells can grow and divide again. When enough cells are present, the cells signal each other to stop growing. Cancer can begin when cells get the wrong signal and continue growing.

Did I really begin life as a single cell?

As hard as it is to imagine, you began life as a single cell when a sperm from your father united with an egg from your mother. Each parent contributed 23 chromosomes to this cell to give you a total of 46 chromosomes. These chromosomes are the "blueprint" for you. They contain the *genes* which carry information for each of your traits. Your chromosomes hold thousands and thousands of genes, and almost all of your body cells have an identical set. Genes tell the cells how to make and shape each tissue and organ in your body. They even determine the color of your skin, eyes, and hair.

Your life began when a sperm from your father fertilized an egg from your mother

At first you were only one cell. Then the cell divided and became two. Each of these cells divided again and again. Cell division continued until you were a ball of thousands of cells. The cells began to specialize for different tasks. Some became blood cells, others nerve cells, skin cells, muscle cells, and so on. For this to happen, some genes in a particular kind of cell needed to work and other genes needed not to work. Scientists have found that cells contain "switches" for turning genes on and off.

Human chromosomes

What is cancer?

A cancer cell is an outlaw. It doesn't obey the "rules" that healthy cells follow. Instead of dividing only when new cells are needed, cancer cells "go wild" and divide continually without any apparent order. They don't necessarily grow *faster* than normal cells, they just ignore the "stop growth" signal and keep growing. They also ignore tissue boundaries and invade neighboring tissue or even spread into distant tissue. Cancer cells tend to be less spe-

cific in their function than normal cells and cannot perform normal cell functions. What makes them so deadly is
that they crowd out normal cells and interfere with many
of the body's normal activities. If they block too many
vital functions, then the body dies.

Cancer takes many forms. There are more than 100
different types of cancer. They are usually named for the
tissue or organ where they begin. Liver cancer starts in the
liver. Bone cancer starts in the bones. Breast cancer always
starts in the breast.

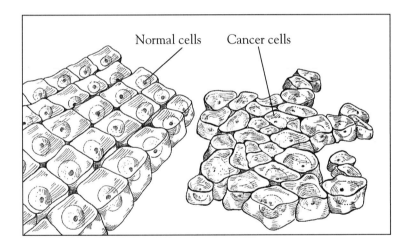

Normal cells   Cancer cells

Why do cells become cancerous?

During cell division chromosomes make exact copies
of themselves. Sometimes something goes wrong. One of
the genes on a chromosome changes or *mutates*. If the
mutation occurs in a growth gene—a gene that controls
cell growth—it can cause the cell to go haywire. The cell
grows and divides when it is not supposed to. This change

becomes permanent in the chromosomes and is passed on to each new cell.

The same result happens if the change occurs in a "turn-off" gene, a gene responsible for turning off growth genes. Think of a mutated "turn-off" gene as a broken switch. With the "turn-off" gene disabled, the growth gene turns on. Cell growth spins out of control.

Gene mutations probably occur most frequently while a cell is dividing. Scientists think that more than one mutation is needed to turn a normal cell into a cancer cell. These mutations could occur over many years.

What is a tumor?

When cells of any kind multiply too fast without any order, they can form a lump or *tumor*. Many people panic when they hear the word tumor. Yet most lumps or tumors are *benign*. That means they are harmless. They are not cancerous and they do not spread to other parts of the body. Benign tumors seldom threaten life. Often they can be surgically removed with the expectation that they won't grow back.

What is a malignant tumor?

A *malignant* tumor is cancerous. It is dangerous because its cells can spread or *metastasize* to other tissues and organs. When a tumor metastasizes, cancer cells break off and travel through the bloodstream or lymph vessels to distant parts of the body. At the new sites they can start another tumor. That is what makes cancer cells so scary.

(The role of the lymph vessels and lymph system is explained on pages 48 and 49.)

How can you make cancer less scary?

Because cancer can spread it is important to find it early in its development before it sends cells to other parts of the body. Fortunately, it is possible to stop the spread of many cancers, including breast cancer, when they are found in their earliest stages.

How do noninvasive cancers differ from invasive cancers?

A *noninvasive* breast cancer is cancer at an early stage. It has formed a very small tumor but has not invaded surrounding tissues. Noninvasive cancers are found in one place and have only a few layers of cells. They are often called *in situ* cancers. The term *in situ* is Latin for still "in the site" where they started.

An *invasive* breast cancer has broken through the borders of surrounding tissue and invaded it. By the time many breast cancers are detected they have become invasive. Doctors often refer to invasive cancers as *infiltrating* cancers.

An invasive cancer is *localized* if it has remained in a single lump and has not spread to distant tissues. An invasive cancer with *regional* involvement has just begun to spread. Its cells may have metastasized to other nearby tissues such as the skin or they may have become trapped by lymph nodes close by. (Lymph nodes are explained on page 46.) In time, invasive cancers will spread to *distant* sites far

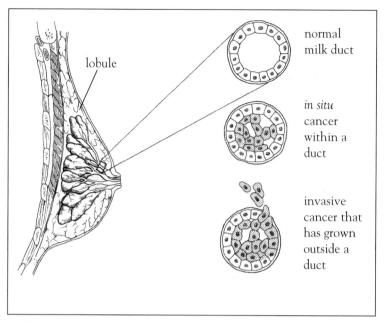

Enlarged view of a milk duct

from the original site. A cancer cell from the breast can travel to the bones, lung, liver, and other parts of the body.

What is the difference between primary cancer and secondary cancer?

A *primary* tumor is the place where cancer first develops. If the cancer spreads to more distant parts of the body, it will form *secondary* tumors. When breast cancer spreads, it is still breast cancer even if it grows in the bones, lungs, or the liver.

What is breast cancer?

Breast cancer is cancer that originates in the breast. There are several different kinds of breast cancer. Almost

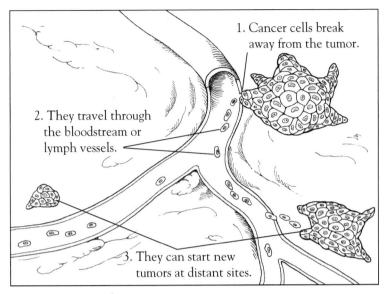

How cancer spreads

all begin in the *epithelial* cells that line the milk ducts and milk sacs. Epithelial cells cover the inside and outside surfaces of organs. Cancers that arise in epithelial cells are called *carcinomas*.

Nearly 90 percent of all breast cancers begin in the milk ducts. Another 5 percent or so start in the lobules. (Milk ducts and lobules were explained on page 16.) The rest develop in the surrounding tissues. These include Paget's disease, a breast cancer that starts in the milk ducts in the nipple and grows out onto the nipple surface, and inflammatory breast cancer, which begins in the ducts and spreads into the lymph vessels of the skin.

Can breast cancer start anywhere in the breast?

About half of all breast cancers form in the upper outer

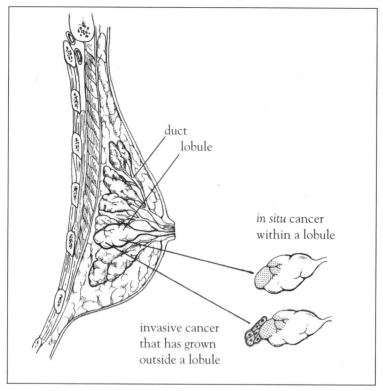

duct
lobule

in situ cancer
within a lobule

invasive cancer
that has grown
outside a lobule

About five percent of all breast cancers start in the lobules

quarter of the breast. This area contains more milk glands than other areas. Another fifth of breast cancers develop around the nipple. This is where all the ducts come together. About 15 percent begin in the upper inner quarter, 11 percent in the outer lower quarter and 6 percent in the inner lower quarter.

What are lymph nodes?

The more you learn about breast cancer the more you will hear the term *lymph nodes*. What exactly are they?

Lymph nodes form part of your body's defense system against germs and other harmful substances. You have plenty of these bean-shaped structures in your neck, armpits, and groin, as well as in other parts of your body. If you have ever had swollen glands, then you have felt swelling in your lymph nodes.

If bacteria slip by your body's first line of defense—your skin—then white blood cells in the lymph system go on a seek and destroy mission to kill them. The lymph nodes filter out germs and poisons to prevent them from entering the bloodstream. The lymph nodes contain *lymphocytes*, a kind of white blood cell that fights infection by producing antibodies.

It may help to think of your white blood cells as cops

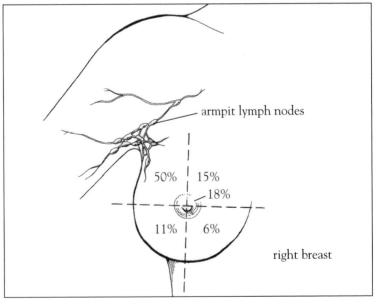

Location of most breast cancers   Statistics source: National Cancer Institute

Lymph nodes in and near the breast

and the lymph nodes as jails. If the bacteria—the bad guys—escape them and enter the blood, then your body's third line of defense springs into action. White blood cells in your blood and spleen launch a fullscale attack. The liver pitches in, too. This third line of defense amounts to calling in the army.

What is the difference between the lymph system and the bloodstream?

To really get a handle on the key role the lymph system plays in the spread of cancer, you need to know how it works. But first we need to look at how your bloodstream, or circulatory system functions because it interacts with the lymph system. Is this beginning to sound too complicated? Stay with me. A lot of this stuff you already learned in school.

How the Circulatory and Lymph Systems Work

CIRCULATORY SYSTEM:

Your heart pumps blood to every part of your body through small tubes called blood vessels. The *arteries* are blood vessels that carry oxygen-rich blood away from the heart to the tissues. They branch into smaller and smaller arteries, finally ending in *capillaries*, the smallest blood vessels. Your capillaries are so narrow, red blood cells must pass through them single file. In the capillaries important exchanges occur between the blood and the body cells. Oxygen and nutrients move through the capillary walls and into the body cells. Carbon dioxide and wastes move from the body cells into the capillaries. The blood from the capillaries then flows into *veins*, the blood vessels that return blood to your heart.

LYMPH SYSTEM:

The lymph system is a second network of tiny tubes. It runs through your body, usually alongside your major veins, and soaks up lymph fluid. The lymph moves into tiny lymph vessels that drain into larger and larger ones. The two biggest lymph vessels empty into two veins near your heart. Lymph nodes cluster at intervals along the lymph vessels. They filter out and destroy bacteria, tumor cells, and other harmful substances picked up by the lymph.

In the breast, lymph vessels lie in the spaces between and around the milk-producing lobes. These vessels connect with lymph nodes in the underarm and lymph nodes next to the breast bone. Lymph from the breast can also drain into lymph nodes near the collarbone and at the side of the neck.

Location of the lymph vessels   *The circulatory system*

Does the lymph system have anything to do with the spread of cancer?

When cancer cells break away from a tumor they may be carried away by lymph fluid or by blood. The nearby lymph nodes go on the defense and filter out the cancer cells. Unfortunately, the nodes may become cancerous themselves.

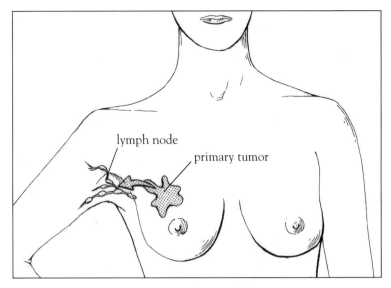

Breast-cancer cells may spread to distant body parts

The most important factor in determining the outlook for a breast-cancer patient is the condition of the lymph nodes. Lymph nodes that are free of cancer are called *negative nodes*. Lymph nodes with cancer are called *positive nodes*.

Positive lymph nodes are a sign that cancer cells were able to move out of the breast and get at least as far as the lymph nodes. The worry is that the cancer cells may also have gone elsewhere in the body. In general, women with negative nodes have a better chance of remaining cancer free than women with positive nodes.

Can you catch breast cancer?

You can't "catch" breast cancer from somebody who has it since there are no breast cancer germs. Breast cancer occurs when something goes wrong with cells in the breast and cell growth runs wild. It develops from cells that were once normal. Medical researchers have not been able to show that viruses cause breast cancer in humans.

No one knows exactly what causes a normal breast cell to become a cancerous cell. It is probably not the work of any one factor, but a result of a group of at least five or six factors that interact with each other. Think of cancer as a baseball team—a mean and vicious baseball team. You can't have a team with only one player; you need lots of players who support each other. Scientists know that the "cancer team" involves chromosomes but they haven't identified the precise role of the other "players."

Scientists have narrowed down the field of cancer-causing candidates:

- A family history of breast cancer.
- The work of female hormones.
- Exposure to radiation or some harmful chemicals.
- Something in our diets.

There is also the possibility that the cause of breast cancer is something not yet identified.

Everybody reacts differently to these cancer-causing candidates. What will trigger breast cancer in one woman will not necessarily trigger breast cancer in another. Some women are born with a damaged gene or genes and may need only a few exposures to cancer-causing agents to make cell growth go haywire. You will learn more about who is at risk in the next chapter, and how to protect yourself from breast cancer in Chapter Four.

Chapter Three:
Who Gets
Breast Cancer?

You have probably heard this scary message: *Breast cancer will strike one in eight women. Those with a family history of the disease face a greater risk.* Both these statements are accurate, but they don't tell the whole story. Without more explanation, they feed into breast cancer hysteria and fail to inform women that breast cancer detected at an early stage can usually be cured.

If you are frightened by the one-in-eight statistic, you are not alone. Many, many women and girls have been scared by it. They look around a crowded room and think, "One out of every eight women here will get breast cancer." And if the frightened individual has a relative with the disease, she may convince herself that she is next.

Some people mistakenly believe the one-in-eight statistic reflects the number of women who have cancer today or who can expect to develop the disease sometime in the near future. The statistic is misleading in another way. It does not mean that at any given moment you, *as a teenager,* have one chance in eight of developing breast cancer. Your risk now is quite low but it will rise as you age. Most breast cancers occur in post menopausal women—women who no longer menstruate.

The one-in-eight odds take into account women who live to age ninety-five or older. An average woman has one chance in eight that she will develop breast cancer in the course of her lifetime. But the risk is not the same at all ages.

What are the odds at different ages?

According to the National Cancer Institute, the odds for a woman getting breast cancer by age twenty-five is only 1 in 19,608! *That means that only 1 woman out of 19,608 women will get breast cancer by the time she is twenty-five.* The odds of breast cancer appearing by age thirty is 1 in 2,525; by age forty, it is 1 in 217; and by age fifty the risk is 1 in 50. *Most women who get breast cancer develop it after age sixty-five.*

But what do all these numbers really say about *your* risk? The statistics may apply to you or they may not. They underestimate the risk for women who have a mother or sister with the disease. They overestimate the risk for women with no family history. In addition, the risk factors for breast cancer may change dramatically between now and the time you enter old age. Researchers have no idea what the risks will be in the future.

No one can say for sure whether or not you will get breast cancer. Because everybody is different, doctors cannot give you an exact answer. It is ironic that medical researchers can observe that one woman in eight will get breast cancer but they cannot reliably identify the women who will get it.

Are all women at risk?

Probably every woman worries about breast cancer at some time. This shouldn't be surprising—*every* woman is at some risk to get it. Approximately 20 percent of all breast cancers develop in women with a family history of the disease. The other 80 percent appear in women with no known family history of it. Your risk of getting breast cancer depends on a variety of factors, which will be discussed shortly. However, even women at higher risk usually have less than a 30 percent chance of developing breast cancer themselves. That means *most* women with a family history of breast cancer will *not* get it themselves.

What causes most breast cancer?

Most breast cancers arise from mutations that take place in breast cells after birth. These mutations cannot be passed from parent to child because they did not occur in a sperm or egg cell—the cells that transmit genetic information from one generation to the next. *Less than 5 percent of breast cancers are caused by a known inherited cancer-causing gene.* This means most breast cancers are not triggered by an inherited gene.

Who is at higher risk to get breast cancer?

Having a mother or sister with breast cancer puts you at greater risk of getting breast cancer, too. So does having an aunt or grandmother with the disease, but not quite as much. The key is whether the cancer appeared before menopause. The earlier cancer appears the more likely it is connected to hereditary factors.

The women at highest risk are those who have two or more close relatives (mother or sisters) with breast cancer. So are women whose mothers or sisters contracted the disease before menopause or had it in both breasts. These women may have a genetic *predisposition* to breast cancer. They may have inherited a defective gene that can trigger breast cancer.

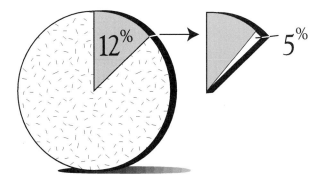

One in eight women will get breast cancer in their life time. Less than five percent of these cancers are due to a known inherited cancer-causing gene.

On the other hand, the older a woman is when breast cancer arises, the less likely it is that the tendency for cancer was inherited. If the cancer occurred after menopause and affected only one breast, it may be a result of mutations in a breast cell that cannot be passed on. If you have a grandmother, aunt, or cousin who developed breast cancer after age fifty-five, you *may* not have an increased risk at all. Even if you have two relatives who developed breast cancer late in life, it could just be a coincidence.

What is a cancer-prone family?

Unfortunately, some women belong to cancer-prone families. In these families a striking pattern emerges. Breast cancer, as well as other kinds of cancer, appears early and moves through the generations. Researchers attribute the cancers to an inherited, defective gene and they have identified several different genes that are the culprits.

One gene, dubbed BRCA1, appears to be responsible for half of all inherited breast cancers. (BRCA1 stands for BReast CAncer gene #1.) Women who carry a mutated form of BRCA1 face as much as an 80 percent chance of developing breast cancer by age sixty-five. They also have an increased chance of getting ovarian cancer (cancer of the ovaries). Researchers estimate that 1 out of every 200 women carry this gene defect.

About one in 200 women carry the BRCA1 gene. Of these women, as many as 80% will develop breast cancer by the time they are 65.

Try not to panic if you belong to a cancer-prone family. You still have a good chance—50 percent—of *not* inheriting the defective gene. Researchers are developing a special blood test to identify carriers of the mutated BRCA1 gene. Perhaps it will be readily available by the time you reach your twenties, and you will be able to know for sure whether or not you are a carrier.

What happens to women identified with a mutated BRCA1 gene?

Today, women who are identified with the defective gene face a difficult choice. Should they undergo a double *mastectomy*—surgery to remove both breasts—or should they continue to live with the risk, along with careful monitoring? This will change in the future. By the time you become an adult, researchers may find a way to beat breast cancer. Women with the BRCA1 will have better options.

How does a cancer-causing gene work?

Researchers believe that in families with hereditary breast cancers, an inherited mutation in one gene makes a woman more likely to develop the disease. The mutation probably appears in a "turn-off" gene—a gene which normally squelches any tendency of a cell to divide wildly. The mutation destroys the gene's ability to prevent uncontrolled cell growth. This mutation can be passed from generation to generation in sperm and egg cells. How?

Remember that humans begin life as a single cell when a sperm from the father unites with an egg from the mother.

Each parent contributes 23 chromosomes to this cell. The chromosomes contain the genes which carry information for each trait. If a gene in a sperm or egg cell mutates, then the mutation will be passed on to the offspring. It will appear in the chromosomes of all the body cells. The offspring has 1 chance in 2 of passing the mutated gene onto the next generation. This means if your mother or father inherited a cancer-causing gene, you have 1 chance in 2 that it was passed on to you. If you inherit a cancer-causing gene, you have a 50-50 chance of transmitting it to each of your children.

For most traits, an individual has two genes—one from the father, one from the mother. An individual with a cancer-causing mutation from one parent will most likely inherit a normal, cancer-suppressing gene for the same trait from the other parent. For the first part of her life, the normal gene prevents cancer growth. For cancer to occur, the normal gene must mutate. The woman must acquire a mutation in one of her breast cells that knocks out or damages the normal gene. This means that even if you inherited a cancer-causing gene from your mother or father, there is a chance that you won't get cancer. In addition, you can take steps to protect yourself against cancer. The next chapter describes what you can do.

Why do inherited cancers usually turn up earlier than noninherited ones?

Inherited breast cancers usually show up earlier than *noninherited* ones because fewer mutations are needed to trigger the cancer. However, even carriers of a defective BRCA1 gene may not have to worry about breast cancer appearing while in their teens. The cancer does not seem to arise until after the age of twenty-five.

Is the frequency of breast cancer increasing?

Breast cancer is the most common cancer among women. The number of women stricken by it has increased dramatically over the past fifty years. In 1940, when breast-cancer statistics were first recorded, there were about 56 cases for every 100,000 women. In 1989, the number was nearly double—about 105 cases for every 100,000 women. That adds up to an astounding 180,000 new cases of breast cancer each year in the United States.

The "good" news, however, is that despite the increase in new cases, the death rate from breast cancer has not increased. It remains steady at 27 deaths for every 100,000 women. That means more women are getting breast cancer, but treatment is successful in more cases. Women are living longer after the disease has been detected and most don't die prematurely from it.

Researchers attribute a recent surge in new cases to better detection methods. More breast cancers were discovered at an earlier stage than could have been picked up previously. If left alone, some of these very early growth— the *in situ* cancers—might never have progressed into full-fledged cancers.

Another cause for the increase in breast cancer can be attributed to increased life expectancy. Women live longer today than in previous generations so more women are around to get the disease. Still, the grim news is that about 46,000 women a year die from breast cancer. Something must be done to bring this number down. You can help by making sure you don't become one of these statistics.

What are risk factors?

Breast cancer is a very complex disorder. It does not have a single cause but has many causes that interact with each other over time. As you already know, in some cancer-prone families, heredity plays a major role. But what else increases the risk? Why are women today more likely to get breast cancer than in the olden days?

Scientists believe that genes can be damaged by exposure to cancer-causing agents in the environment. For example, cigarette smoke clearly has a hand in the onset of lung cancer. If you smoke, you increase your risk of getting lung cancer. Sunlight is linked to skin cancer. If you sunbathe frequently, you increase your risk for skin cancer.

You can protect yourself from lung cancer and skin cancer by not smoking, by avoiding prolonged exposure to the sun, and by using sunscreen. Protecting yourself against breast cancer, however, is not as easy. The risk factors for breast cancer are not as clear-cut except for one and it is unavoidable.

Did you know that the greatest risk factor for you and all other girls and women is your sex? Some men get breast cancer. However, having female hormones increases the risk of breast cancer. That is why the vast majority of people with breast cancer are women, not men. It seems so unfair!

Other possible risk factors include environmental pollutants and radiation. Lifestyle choices such as a poor diet and drinking alcohol may also have a strong effect upon your chance of getting breast cancer.

How can female hormones be a risk factor since they occur naturally?

During each menstrual cycle, a woman experiences hormonal surges. In the first part of the cycle, estrogen rises and then falls; in the second part, progesterone peaks and then wanes. This ebb and flow of hormones stimulates the growth of breast cells.

The chromosomes of breast cells may be more vulnerable to mutation-causing agents during cell division than at other times. If a harmful chemical appears during rapid cell growth, it is more likely to damage the chromosomes, and that could lead to breast cancer later. This means female hormones alone are not cancer-causing agents. But they are cancer-promoting agents. They set the stage for cancer to occur and they can fuel the growth of cancer cells. Think of it this way: *Female hormones are to breast cancer what fertilizer is to plants.*

The longer a woman is exposed to monthly hormonal changes, the greater her risk of developing breast cancer. Women who begin menstruating before age twelve have a *slightly* greater chance of developing breast cancer than those who started their first periods at a later age. Don't panic if you got your period early. Remember, your risk has increased only very, very slightly. Women with a late menopause—after age fifty-five—also have a slightly increased likelihood of developing breast cancer than women with an earlier menopause. There is some suspicion that women who take additional estrogen hormones after menopause have a higher risk of breast cancer than those who do not take estrogen.

When is breast tissue most susceptible to harmful mutations?

Doctors suspect that breast tissue is especially sensitive to harmful mutations during breast development—from the beginning of puberty to the birth of a first child. Pregnancy hormones cause the breast to complete its development. They transform breast cells somehow and make them less likely to mutate. Women who have their first child after age thirty, or who have never given birth, remain more vulnerable to harmful mutations for a longer period than women who have a baby while in their teens or twenties.

This may explain why women who give birth in their teens have *slightly* less chance of getting breast cancer later in life than women who give birth for the first time after the age of thirty. This doesn't mean you should rush to have a baby in your teens or early twenties. The slightly lower risk gained by delaying childbirth isn't significant enough to justify bearing a baby before you are ready.

Women have always had periods. What makes the difference nowadays?

Lifestyle changes that affect the reproductive system may be one of the major reasons behind soaring breast cancer rates. Fifty years ago the average age for starting menstruation was 12 to 13 years and the average age at which a women had her first born was 21 to 22 years. That meant the typical woman was exposed to monthly hormonal changes for only *nine* years or so before her breast cells were matured by pregnancy hormones and became less likely to mutate. Nowadays, the average woman begins to menstruate between ages 11 and 12 and may delay childbearing until she is in her late twenties or thirties. Her exposure to hormone surges lasts about *twenty* years before her breast cells fully mature.

Family planning may also play a role in increasing breast-cancer risk. Women today give birth to fewer children than women did before the advent of birth control. Pregnancy and nursing interrupt the menstrual cycle and decrease exposure to fluctuating hormone levels. In the olden days, bearing five to nine children was the norm. The more children a woman had, the less her body was exposed to hormonal changes. So, how much difference does this make? If you start menstruating at age twelve, give birth to two babies later, nurse them, and stop menstruating at age fifty-one, you will have more than 400 periods. Compare this to your female ancestors who lived one hundred years ago. Most likely their periods started at age 15 or 16, they married in their teens, and they gave birth to many children and nursed them. Your ancestors may have had only a small fraction of the periods that you can expect to have in your lifetime.

Don't let all these statistics on periods and estrogen make you fearful of your own hormones. *About 60 or 70 percent of all breast cancers cannot be explained by estrogen and other known risk factors.* Besides, living in the "good old days" wasn't that healthy. The average person didn't live as long then as the average person does now. For example, in 1920, the life expectancy for a baby girl was about 54 years. The life expectancy for a baby girl born in 1990 is almost 79 years.

Does "the pill" cause cancer?

To avoid unwanted pregnancy, millions of women in industrialized societies such as the United States use some form of birth control during sexual intercourse. Many of these women take birth-control pills to prevent *ovulation*—the release of an egg every month. (If no egg is released, there can be no baby even if a woman has sex.) Different varieties of "the pill" exist and the way they work is quite complicated. Most contain both estrogen and progesterone, the hormones that control the female reproductive cycle.

The pill is easy to use. Starting on the fifth day of a period, a woman takes a hormone-containing pill every day for twenty-one days to block ovulation. For the next seven days she takes no pills (or she takes dummy pills—

with no hormones). This makes her hormone levels fall and her period come. *A word of caution about the pill. While it does prevent pregnancy, it does not stop the spread of AIDS or other sexually-transmitted diseases.* Several studies have explored a possible connection between the pill and breast cancer. Some investigations performed in the early 1980s found evidence of a link. More recent studies, however, have not. The conflicting results may be due to changes in the pill itself.

In the late 1960s and early 1970s when the pill first came out, it contained much higher amounts of estrogen and progesterone than it does today. Women who used it between the ages of twenty and thirty increased their risk of getting breast cancer. These women are now in their forties and fifties.

Today, the pill uses much lower hormone doses than the earlier version. It probably poses little breast-cancer risk to most women. However, some doctors warn young women at high risk for breast cancer to avoid the pill.

When the time comes for you to think about birth control, you will need to discuss the options with your nurse or physician. If you have a family history of breast cancer, the pill may not be the safest birth-control method for you.

Is there a birth-control pill that will prevent breast cancer?

Researchers hope to develop a new kind of birth-control pill that will prevent pregnancy and prevent breast cancer. They are working on a pill that contains gonadotropin-releasing hormones, a hormone that stops the body from producing most of its estrogen and progesterone. The pill works as a birth-control pill because it prevents the release of an egg. It lessens the risk of breast cancer by cutting off the signaling system that causes breast cells to divide during a normal menstrual cycle. If successful, this pill may be available by the year 2000.

Is there a link between a high-fat diet and breast cancer?

American women are five times more likely to get breast cancer than women in China and Japan. However, Chinese and Japanese women who move to America increase their likelihood of getting breast cancer. Their American-born daughters face an even greater risk.

In the 1980s scientists sought an explanation. A high-fat diet seemed to be a likely suspect because the American diet is laced with chips, French fries, fatty meats, and ice cream, and the diet in Asia is not. Yet, in a major study of the eating habits of nearly 90,000 American nurses, researchers could not find evidence that linked breast cancer to *adult* women who eat high-fat diets.

This study didn't investigate the impact of a truly low-fat diet on breast-cancer prevention. A high-fat diet in adult women may not contribute to their breast cancer risk but it certainly isn't doing anything to decrease it. Perhaps a truly low-fat diet may help in preventing breast cancer. This needs to be investigated by scientists.

Don't use the findings of the nurses' study as an excuse to eat a lot of greasy foods. It is possible that a high-fat diet during *adolescence* may increase breast-cancer risk. After all, your teenage years are the time when breast tissue grows most rapidly.

Researchers have begun to study the possibility of a link between breast cancer and a teenage diet high in fat. Their findings won't do you much good, however. They'll come out about the time you have teenage daughters or even granddaughters!

Do overweight women face a greater breast cancer risk?

Obese young women actually have a slightly *lower* risk of developing breast cancer than others because they tend to get their periods less frequently. They have lower estrogen levels than average and this probably puts them at less risk.

This is not a reason to overeat and pack on weight. After menopause, overweight women have a slightly *higher* risk of developing breast cancer. Body fat produces estrogen so even after the ovaries shut down for good, obese women still have some estrogen circulating in their bodies.

Do all groups of women face the same risk?

All women worldwide are at risk to get breast cancer but it is more common in women from North America and Northern Europe, and in women who rank above average in income and education. Within the United States, native Hawaiian women and women of European-Jewish descent face an increased risk. African-American women, Native American women, and women of Chinese, Japanese, Filipino, or Mexican descent have a lower risk than white women. Although African-American women are less likely to get breast cancer than white women, they are more likely to die from it if they get it. This is probably a result of inferior health care among poor African-American women.

The regions in the United States with the highest rate of breast-cancer cases are the northeast and mid-Atlantic regions. Researchers suspect that environmental factors may be responsible and they are investigating areas where breast-cancer cases are higher than average.

Don't have a panic attack if you fall into one of these groups! Your risk is only *slightly* increased, and the next chapter tells you how you can protect yourself.

Can men get breast cancer?

Breast cancer can strike men but it is a rare occurrence. Only 300 men die of it each year in the United States. Interestingly, men who carry the defective BRCA1 gene are *not* at increased risk to develop breast cancer. However, they may be at higher risk for developing prostate cancer. (The prostate is a male sex gland located near the bladder.) Men who have a family history of *male* breast cancer are at higher risk of getting breast cancer themselves.

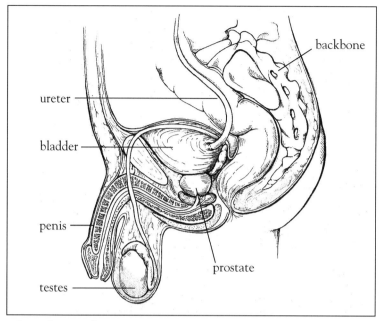

The male reproductive system

Will I get breast cancer if my breasts are bumped or fondled?

Breast cancer is *not* caused by bumping or bruising the breast. Touching or fondling the breasts does *not* cause breast cancer either. Letting a boy caress or kiss your breasts will not give you breast cancer, but other good reasons exist for not engaging in this type of behavior until you are mature. The powerful feelings this behavior can evoke can lead to intercourse before you are emotionally ready.

How does radiation trigger cancer?

Radiation can damage chromosomes by mutating genes

or rearranging them. Diagnostic X-rays are probably the most likely source of radiation exposure for you. The amount of radiation you receive from a single medical X-ray is quite small and probably not dangerous in itself. However, women who have radiation therapy for other cancers, such as Hodgkin's Disease, face an increased risk of getting breast cancer because they receive at least one-hundred-thousand times more radiation during the course of their therapy than they would receive in a normal chest X-ray. It takes a long time—sometimes twenty or more years—for cancer caused by radiation to appear.

Is our environment hazardous?

Since the majority of breast cancers cannot be explained by estrogen and other known risk factors, researchers are trying to pinpoint other triggers. Many scientists believe that toxins (poisons) in the environment may play a significant role in the soaring breast-cancer rate. Some toxins are harmful chemicals whose effects on chromosomes are similar to those of radiation—they can mutate and rearrange genes. Others encourage the growth of tumors. Like radiation, the effects of toxins often show up decades after exposure.

One suspect is DDT, a banned pesticide. DDT came into widespread use after World War II to combat insects. It acts like estrogen and encourages rapid cell growth. DDT may pose much less risk to you than to the women of your mother's generation who were exposed to it between 1945 and 1972, when it was banned in the United States.

Studies in Israel have shown that when DDT use is eliminated, breast-cancer rates drop.

Is DDT the only harmful chemical in the environment?

DDT is probably not the only environmental villain. Although DDT is no longer marketed in the United States, other pesticides in use today may be just as dangerous. Some researchers think *endosulfan*, a pesticide used widely on fruits and vegetables, may have the same estrogen-like effect on the body as DDT. The safety of endosulfan and other pesticides is coming under close scrutiny as scientists try to establish a connection between pesticides and breast cancer. PCBs (formerly used to insulate electrical components) may also be harmful. They have long been suspected cancer-causing agents but convincing proof is lacking.

Scientists are currently exploring links between breast cancer and other environment hazards, including vehicle exhaust, contaminated drinking water, contaminated landfills, and chemicals formed in food by high-temperature cooking. Investigators are even looking into the effect of the electric fields given off by power lines and electrical appliances. In the next chapter you will learn how to reduce your exposure to suspected cancer-causing agents and promoters.

What doesn't cause breast cancer?

Cancer cannot be caused by touching your breasts or letting somebody else touch, kiss, or suck them. Bumping or bruising your breasts will not cause cancer. Neither will nursing a baby.

If a pregnant woman has breast cancer, she cannot pass it onto her unborn child. If a nursing mother has breast cancer she cannot give it to her baby through the milk. You cannot get breast cancer from thinking and worrying about it. You cannot catch it by kissing or touching somebody with it, or eating the food they prepare.

I think I am at higher risk for breast cancer. How can I stop being so scared?

Remember that *all* women are at risk for breast cancer but many fail to realize it. They think breast cancer won't happen to them, so they don't take precautions. If these women develop the disease, they may detect it at such an advanced stage that it cannot easily be cured. You have an advantage. You know you will need to monitor your breasts as you grow older. If you develop the disease you will probably find it at such an early stage that it can be cured easily. Chapter Four explains how you can help yourself.

Chapter Four:
Improving Your Odds

By now (if you have read much of the first three chapters), you probably have questions of your own—like these:

If breast cancer mainly affects older women, why do teenagers need to think about it?

If the exact cause of breast cancer escapes medical researchers, how can I hope to avoid it?

Is there anything I can do to improve my odds of preventing breast cancer?

If these and other questions gnaw at you, read on!

Experts think the American lifestyle is partly responsible for the high rate of cancer in this country. You may be able to lower your risk of breast cancer by making healthy lifestyle choices. These choices include eating a low-fat diet, exercising regularly, and steering away from alcohol. All are described in the following pages.

Does what I eat make a difference?

Wouldn't it be great to blame breast cancer on American eating habits? Then you could simply avoid foods that are bad for you and eat only the good stuff. Researchers are attempting to do just that. They are seeking not only the foods that may increase risk but they are also trying to identify foods that can protect against breast cancer, too. So far they have had mixed results.

Right now, the link between diet and breast cancer resembles a big jigsaw puzzle with a lot of pieces missing. As you grow older, researchers will undoubtedly discover more of the puzzle parts. Someday they will fully understand the role of diet in breast cancer. For now, the jumble of puzzle pieces provides strong clues, but no definite answers. These clues will be your guide for increasing your protection against breast cancer.

What's all the concern about fat?

Studies show that a diet high in fat may lead to higher estrogen levels in the body. You already know that estrogen sets the stage for cancer by causing breast cells to divide. So anything that elevates the level of estrogen is not good news.

Some researchers think that a high-fat diet during childhood may be the reason girls today begin to menstruate earlier than in previous generations. It may speed up sexual development and increase the level of estrogen in the bloodstream. One study in the Netherlands showed that a low-fat, high-fiber diet slowed breast development.

Why not eliminate fat totally from the diet?

Fat is an important nutrient. Your body uses it mainly for energy but also requires it in small quantities for growth and repair of damaged tissue. Fat insulates against cold and protects vital body parts from injury. To stay healthy, you must include some fat in your diet.

Are all fats the same?

Fats can be divided into two large groups. The ones that are *solid* at room temperature contain mainly *saturated* fatty acids. The fats that are *liquid* at room temperature contain *unsaturated* fatty acids. The difference lies in their chemical makeup and how they affect our health. If you are interested in science you might appreciate the chemical distinction—saturated fatty acids contain a greater amount of hydrogen atoms than unsaturated fatty acids.

Saturated fat comes mainly from animal fats, solid vegetable shortenings, margarines, and most dairy products. Try to minimize your intake of these foods. Vegetable oils such as canola, olive, soybean, corn, and sunflower oils make good sources of unsaturated fats which are better for you. Olive oil may be particularly good for you.

Are some fats really good for me?

Oils containing omega-3 fatty acids may protect against the development of breast cancer. Fatty fish such as salmon, tuna, rainbow trout, mackerel, sable, whitefish, herring, and sardines provide an excellent source of omega-3 containing oils. Do you like to eat a lot of these

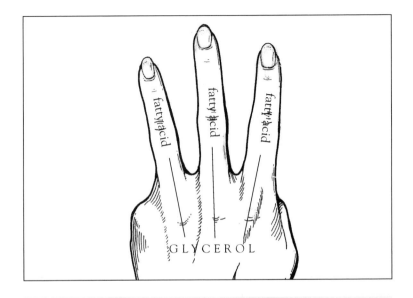

Diagram of a Fat Molecule[1]

Most molecules of fat consist of three fatty-acids molecules joined to one glycerol molecule. To picture a fat molecule, make a fist and then extend the fingers on one hand. Imagine the knuckles at the bottom of each of your three fingers as a skeleton of carbon atoms—the backbone of the fat molecule. This backbone is called *glycerol.*

Think of each finger as a chain of carbon atoms with hydrogen atoms attached. These fingers are the three fatty acids that make up the fat molecule. Just as your fingers are slightly different, so fatty acids vary. They can be long or short, straight or curvy. They can be filled with hydrogen atoms or have a few empty spaces. Saturated fatty acids contain all the hydrogen atoms they can hold. Unsaturated fatty acids have room for more.

1. Adapted with permission from an idea by Dr. Joyce A. Nettleton in *Seafood and Health* (Huntington, NY: Osprey Books, 1987), p. 23.

The omega-3 fatty acids found in salmon, tuna, and other fatty fish may protect against cancer

fish? To obtain benefits from them scientists recommend that you consume two or three servings a week.

Why should I worry about fats now?

As a teenager, your breasts are especially sensitive to harmful chemicals during rapid cell growth. Estrogen encourages this rapid growth and high-fat diets increase estrogen. A truly low-fat diet with plenty of fiber may actually *decrease* the amount of estrogen in your body and protect you against breast cancer.

In the United States fat accounts for a whopping 36

percent of the daily calories for the average woman. Most of the fat comes from animals: beef, pork, lamb, poultry, eggs, and dairy products. Although the fat comes from different sources, the typical American eats the equivalent of a stick of butter a day!

In Japan, where breast-cancer rates are much lower, fat supplies only 10 to 20 percent of the calories in a typical diet. Little of it comes from meat.

Experts suggest that Americans lower the total amount of fat in their diets and try to avoid saturated fats. Here are some ways to reduce the amount of fat you eat:

- Cut down on fried and oily foods (including French fries and chips).
- Switch to skim or low-fat dairy products.
- Substitute poultry, fish, and lean meats for red meats streaked with fat.
- Remove skin from chicken and turkey before eating.
- Minimize the amount of salad dressing, butter, margarine, and rich sauces that you add to food.
- Cut down on packaged snacks and baked goodies such as cakes and cookies.

Is it possible that fat isn't the problem?

Some researchers question whether fat deserves the blame for the rise in breast cancer. They wonder if the effects linked to fat may simply be due to a diet high in total calories. Eskimo women traditionally eat a high-fat diet and have almost no breast cancer.

Other researchers point to DDT and other toxic pollutants that collect in fat. People who eat a high-fat diet most likely take in greater amounts of these poisons than people who maintain a low-fat diet.

Some experts think fiber holds the key. They believe eating more fiber—not less fat—will reduce breast-cancer risk. Fiber consists mostly of the remains of plant-cell walls. All fruits, vegetables, beans, and grains contain some fiber but our bodies cannot digest it. Its main effect is to move food and stool through the large intestine and out of the body. Some researchers think that a diet rich in fiber may protect against breast cancer by increasing the excretion (elimination) of estrogen through bowel movements.

To get the fiber you need, eat plenty of fruits and vegetables. Don't bother to peel the skins from potatoes and apples, peaches, plums, and other similar fruits. The skins contain lots of fiber. Put peas and beans on your weekly menu, and choose breads, pasta, and cereals made from bran or whole grains.

Was President Bush wrong about broccoli?

When George Bush lived in the White House he made headlines by disclosing his dislike of broccoli. If you share his feelings, perhaps this may convert you into a broccoli lover: Broccoli contains one chemical which breaks down estrogen in the body and one or more chemicals that fortify cells against tumors.

Cabbage, Brussels sprouts, cauliflower, radishes, bok choy, collards, kale, turnips, and other foods in the cabbage family also contain these chemicals. Perhaps eating foods from the cabbage family will help prevent breast cancer. Interestingly, Asian women eat large quantities of these vegetables and they experience lower rates of breast cancer. Try to eat several servings of these foods each week.

Vegetables in the cabbage family

What other foods can protect against breast cancer?

Researchers think fruits and vegetables rich in Vitamin E, Vitamin C, and beta-carotene may offer some insurance. These protectors go by the fancy chemical name of *antioxidants*.

Legumes—beans, peas, soybeans, and lentils—may be particularly beneficial. Hispanic women traditionally eat a diet high in fat and loaded with beans. Yet their breast-cancer rate remains lower than that of non-Hispanic white women. Soybeans may help to account for the low breast cancer rates of Japanese women. Women in Japan consume large amounts of tofu (soybean curd) and other soy-based foods.

What exactly is beta-carotene?

Beta-carotene is a yellow particle—a pigment—found in the cells of brightly colored fruits and vegetables. It helps provide the coloring for carrots, peaches, cantaloupes, sweet potatoes, and other produce. Beta-carotene does more than make fruits and vegetables look pretty. Scientists think that it safeguards against cancer.

Beta-carotene plays another important role. Your body converts it to Vitamin A which helps your eyes detect light. You may have been told to eat carrots because they are good for the eyes. Did you think you'd ever be told to eat them because they are good for your breasts?

How can I make healthier food choices?

By now you have probably figured out that switching to a low-fat, high-fiber diet with plenty of fish, beans, fruits, olive oil, soybeans, broccoli, and other vegetables is your best bet for reducing your odds of developing breast cancer. But the task may seem overwhelming. What is a girl to do?

The Food Guide Pyramid shown here can help. The Pyramid makes it easy to choose and follow a healthy eating program. It tells you the number of servings to eat each day from the various food groups.

FOOD GUIDE PYRAMID
A Guide to Daily Food Choices

Fats, Oils & Sweets
Use sparingly

Milk, Yogurt
& Cheese Group
2-3 Servings

Meats, Poultry, Fish,
Dry Beans, Eggs,
& Nuts Group
2-3 Servings

Vegetable
Group
**3-5
Servings**

Fruit Group
2-4 Servings

Bread, Cereal,
Rice, & Pasta
Group
**6-11
Servings**

Source: U.S. Department of Agriculture / U.S. Department of Health and Human Services

Making the switch to healthier eating may seem overwhelming. But the more you know about food and nutrition the easier it will be to make the transition. Ask your librarian to recommend *new* books on nutrition that reflect the Food Guide Pyramid. For more about the Food Guide Pyramid and other nutrition information, see *Further Reading* on pages 178-180.

Why bother to eat a sensible diet if scientists haven't proven it will protect against breast cancer?

Many researchers believe that it is only a matter of time before the link between diet and breast cancer will be demonstrated. In the meantime, a healthy diet can't hurt. Eating sensibly will help you feel and perform at your peak. It will also help to protect you against other forms of cancer, heart disease, and many illnesses.

Should I join a diet support group?

If you are overweight, a diet support group, such as Weight Watchers®, may be beneficial. These groups provide emotional support for weight-watchers. The leaders and other members understand about the temptation to binge on foods like potato chips or ice cream. They will share their own strategies for reining in their appetites.

These groups also give valuable advice on how to plan meals and snacks. Many of their members lose weight but some gain it back later. The main long-term benefit of these groups is they teach you how to reduce the fat in your diet and make healthier food choices.

Will exercise help?

Women who regularly engage in vigorous exercise throughout their lives experience lower rates of breast, ovarian, and uterine cancer. To improve your odds, pick an exercise and stick with it at least three times a week for a minimum of twenty minutes. You can choose from cycling, jogging, skating, swimming, hiking, cross-country skiing, aerobic dancing, and so on. Even a habit of taking brisk walks may make a difference.

You probably have been bombarded with other good reasons to exercise regularly: It strengthens the heart, lungs, and muscles, keeps joints flexible, and reduces body fat when combined with a sensible diet. Did you know exercise provides an added bonus?

It makes you feel better by reducing anxiety and depression. Perhaps you have heard of a "runner's high"? It occurs during exercise when the body releases a chemical that gives a feeling of well-being. Swimmers, bicyclists, and other athletes experience this good feeling, too.

Is there a link between alcohol and breast cancer?

Many excellent reasons exist for teenagers to avoid alcohol and by now you probably think you have heard them all. Alcohol can harm your health and dull your performance in school. It can impair your ability to make good decisions. Drinking and driving often result in traffic accidents. Drinking and operating a boat can end up in tragedy, too. Teenage drinking can lead to alcoholism. Mixing alcohol and other drugs can multiply the nasty effects, causing a harmful overdose, and perhaps, death.

If none of these reasons have convinced you to avoid alcohol, perhaps this will. Drinking alcohol—beer, wine, or hard liquor—increases the risk of breast cancer, especially for women under thirty. The more you drink, the greater your risk.

Is there a link between cigarette smoking and breast cancer?

If you begin smoking heavily in your early teens, you increase your risk of getting breast cancer later in life. The harmful chemicals in cigarette smoke may be the villains. Interestingly, women who begin to smoke at age twenty-five have no increased breast-cancer risk, but like all people who smoke, they have an increased risk of lung cancer and heart disease. What does this mean for you? Don't smoke!

If you can't prevent breast cancer, what can you do about it?

Right now there are no foolproof methods for preventing breast cancer. However, screening techniques exist to find the disease at the earliest possible stage. These techniques include the breast self-exam, the clinical breast exam, and the mammogram. They are all explained in this chapter.

What is the breast self-exam?

The *breast self-exam*, called *BSE* for short, is one of your keys to breast-cancer detection. It is an examination of your breasts that you do yourself.

You need to become familiar with the appearance and feel of your breasts. If you haven't done a BSE before, don't be surprised to find that your breasts feel more like lumpy oatmeal than smooth Jell-O®. The idea of the BSE is to know your breasts so well that you can detect something unusual. As a teenager, the chances of your finding anything out of the ordinary is extremely low. But if you make BSE a lifetime habit, it may save your life when you are older. You should repeat the BSE once a month, about a week after your period begins. This is the time when your breasts are least likely to be swollen or tender, and are the least lumpy.

How do I perform a breast exam?

1. Undress from the waist up and lie flat on your back in bed. Place a pillow under your left shoulder.

2. Raise your left arm behind your head. Use the middle three fingers of your right hand to feel your left breast. Start at the outer edge of your breast, just under the armpit. Press down firmly with the pads of your fingers—the part where the fingerprints are, not the fingertips. Make little dime-sized circles. Gradually, move the little circles around the outside of the breast in a big circle that goes up to your collarbone and then back to where you started.

3. When you return to the beginning, move your fingers about three-quarters of an inch in toward the nipple. Making little circles, work your way around the breast again, in a spiral. Continue until you reach the nipple. Make sure you cover all parts of the breast.

4. Then place the pillow under your right shoulder and repeat the exam on your right breast.

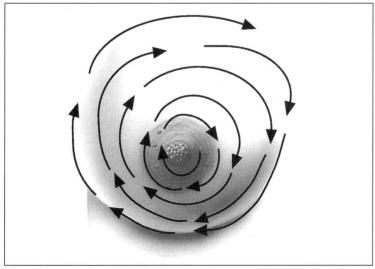

Are there other ways to check your breasts?

Some women find that the spiral pattern doesn't work well for them. They can check their breasts better by substituting a vertical pattern for the spiral in steps 2 and 3. To use a vertical pattern, imagine that you have lines drawn up and down on your breasts, about three-quarters of an inch apart. Beginning at your armpit, work your way straight down in small circles. At the bottom, move over three-quarters of an inch to the next "line" and make your way back up. Repeat this until you have covered the entire breast.

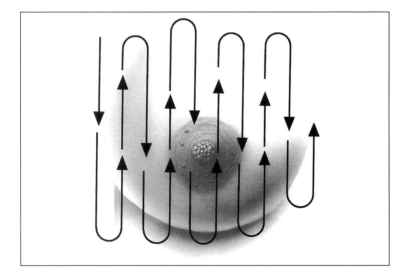

There is still another technique that you can use instead of the spiral or vertical patterns. Imagine that your breast is a pie that has been divided into eight pieces. Making small circles, exam each wedge from the outer edge of the breast in toward the nipple. Go back and forth

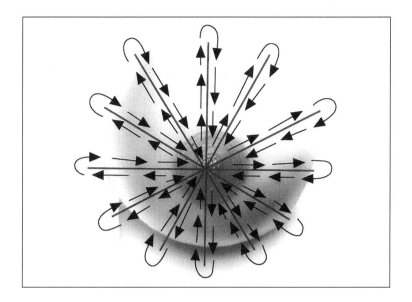

within each wedge to cover all parts of it. Then proceed to the next one. Continue until you have checked out the entire breast.

Is one technique better than the others?

No. Use the technique that best helps you check out your breasts. It may take you several months to become familiar with your breasts and their normal lumpiness. What counts is that you develop the habit of regular breast self-exams.

Don't be alarmed if your breasts change during the month. Remember that the hormonal changes which control your periods also affect the breasts. They may cause a little swelling and tenderness in the breast tissue. Sometimes your breasts may feel heavier, lumpier, or more painful in one month than another. Because of the monthly variation in your breasts, it is important to perform a BSE at the same time every month in your cycle.

Can I perform a breast self-exam in the shower or tub?

You may find it easier to perform a BSE when you bathe. If you make your fingers soapy they can glide over your breast more easily. Just put your left arm behind your head and use your right hand to examine your left breast in the same way you did lying down. Remember to check both breasts.

What am I looking for in a breast self-exam?

After you learn what your breasts feel like normally, you will be looking for a *new* lump or two among the usual lumps. What you are checking for is a distinct lump that feels unusual like a piece of gravel, a marble, or a grape. If you find an unusual lump don't panic! Most lumps found by women—young and old—are harmless. For your peace of mind report it to your nurse or doctor. You need to find out what kind of lump it is.

If an unusual lump isn't cancer, what is it?

Most new lumps that women find during a BSE are not cancerous or even dangerous. Four kinds of *harmless* lumps can be found:

1. **Cysts.** You probably have heard of cysts. These harmless lumps are merely fluid-filled sacs. They feel soft and round and are movable. Their size often changes with the menstrual cycle. Cysts rarely appear in

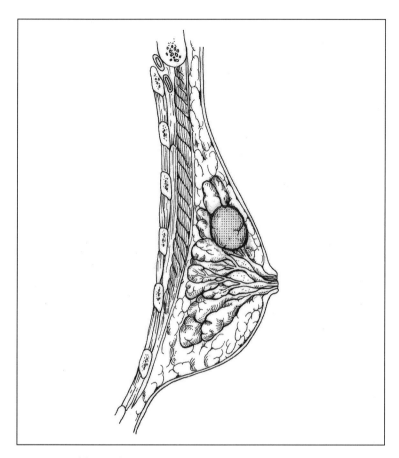

An unusual breast lump

teenagers or young women but middle-aged women near menopause are prone to them.

2. **Fibroadenoma.** Some smooth, round lumps have a scary-sounding name—*fibroadenoma*. They can feel rubbery, or hard like marbles. They crop up mainly in teenagers and young women. They occur more often in black women than white women. The good news is that these solid lumps are not dangerous.

3. **Infections.** Some lumps signal an infection. For example, lumps under the armpit can be swollen lymph glands, similar to the kind you may get in your neck when you experience a sore throat. A painful, red swelling in the breast of a nursing mother is a symptom of a bacterial infection of the milk ducts and glands. Antibiotics can cure it.

4. **Wartlike growths.** Wartlike growths can appear in the milk ducts near the nipple. One sign of them is bleeding from the nipple. They usually occur in women between 45 and 50 years old.

Why does it seem so hard for me to do a breast self-exam?

Many girls and women feel uncomfortable touching their breasts. Some dread the BSE because they fear the discovery of a lump. Others avoid it because they mistakenly think it the same as "playing with yourself." Most women who perform the BSE find it reassuring because they never find a cancerous lump. They feel safe when nothing unusual turns up.

The first few times you do a BSE you may feel uneasy. Breasts are naturally lumpy and every lump may feel like a tumor to you. You may convince yourself that you have cancer! This is a normal reaction but don't use it as an excuse to shy away from the BSE.

Right now, you don't know what is normal for your breasts. You need to learn what's "right" inside your breasts so you can tell if and when something goes wrong. The more you perform the BSE the sooner you will find out what feels right. You will become more confident and the BSE will become less frightening.

If performing a BSE makes you very anxious, you may find it helpful to discuss your worries with your nurse or physician. Your health-care provider will help you learn what "normal" feels like. You may feel embarrassed to do this but your doctor or nurse will be quite familiar with these concerns about BSE, and you will probably feel much better afterward.

Why should I do a breast self-exam if the odds of a teenager getting breast cancer are very low?

Although the occurrence of breast cancer in women below the age of twenty-five is rare—one case in 19,608 women—it can still happen. So why take chances? Breast care should be as natural a part of your life as brushing your teeth or shampooing your hair.

What is a clinical breast exam?

Another important way to detect breast cancer early is the clinical breast exam. A clinical breast exam is similar to the breast self-exam only it is performed by a nurse or physician. Some young women (and older women, too!) feel uncomfortable or embarrassed to have their breasts touched by others in this way. Yet the clinical exam is very thorough and may detect lumps that you missed yourself.

Women between twenty and forty should have a clinical breast exam during their regular checkups once a year or so. Women at higher risk for breast cancer may have them done more frequently—about every six months. Since breast cancer is so rare among teenagers, most doctors don't recommend clinical breast exams for them.

Who is the best doctor or nurse to examine me?

The best doctor or nurse to check you is someone who has experience with breast cancer. This may be a surgical oncologist, gynecologist, nurse practitioner, or any other nurse or physician who specializes in women's health care. If your health-care provider makes you feel uncomfortable, find one who puts you more at ease. You have the right to choose your own nurse or doctor. After all, it's *your* body!

What is a mammogram?

A *mammogram* is a special low-dose X-ray of the breast. It gives a clear, detailed picture of breast tissue. Mammograms provide an excellent way of finding tumors too small to be felt by you or your doctor. Detecting tumors when they are small is extremely important. Breast cancer is more easily cured when discovered early. If a suspicious spot shows up on a mammogram, a biopsy must be performed to determine if it is cancerous or not. Biopsies are explained on page 106.

Mammograms are not perfect. They miss about 10 percent of cancerous tumors because some cancers have the

Small
Cancer·Non·palpable

An actual mammogram showing a small lump

same density as the surrounding breast tissue. These cancers don't show up on the X-ray. For this reason, mammograms don't work as well with younger women. Younger women tend to have denser breast tissue than older women. Ultrasound and MRI may be able to find tumors that mammograms fail to detect. These two methods are explained in the next chapter.

Cancers that mammograms miss usually form lumps and can be detected during a clinical exam. Thus, mammograms, together with clinical breast exams, provide the best tools to save lives today. They will not prevent breast cancer but they can increase the chance of finding the cancer early. Breast cancer can be beaten if you find it early enough.

When should I have a mammogram?

Not enough studies have been done to show the importance of mammograms for women under fifty. As a result, experts differ on their opinions about it. The American Cancer Society recommends that *all* women between the ages of forty and forty-nine have a mammogram done every one to two years. Because cancer risk rises with age, they advise all women age fifty and older to get yearly mammograms.

The National Cancer Institute recommends that women fifty or older get mammograms every one to two years. They advise women between forty and forty-nine to discuss with their doctors whether they should have one or not. The National Cancer Institute will review its guidelines as more studies become available.

The guidelines of the American Cancer Society and the National Center Institute are basically for women who do *not* have a family history of breast cancer. Women whose mothers or sisters developed breast cancer should go for their first mammogram at age thirty-five, or 10 to 15 years earlier than the age at which their relative discovered it—whichever is earlier. That means if your mother detected her breast cancer at age forty-four, you should have your first mammogram by age thirty-four. Check with your doctor about the best time for you to start regular mammograms. Perhaps by the time you are old enough to need one, better screening techniques will be available.

Are breast self exams and mammograms worth the fuss?

- The average lump revealed by regular yearly or bi-yearly mammograms is 1/8 inch. Lumps this size can't be picked up by breast exams.
- The average lump found by a *first* mammogram is 1/4 inch. Lumps this size could still be easily missed during a breast exam.
- The average lump discovered during a regular monthly BSE is 5/8 inch. Many of these lumps could have been detected years earlier with a mammogram.
- The average lump spotted during an occasional BSE is 1 inch.
- The average lump found by women who don't perform BSE is 1 1/2 inches.

What is cystic disease?

"Fibrocystic disease" is not a disease. It is a catch-all term that means different things to different doctors. Some use it to describe women with noncancerous lumps such as cysts, fibroadenomas, wartlike growths, and benign tumors. Others use it to refer to women with noticeably lumpy breasts. The lumpiness typically changes with the menstrual cycle. Sometimes the breasts are tender or sore. This "condition" describes the breasts of at least half of all

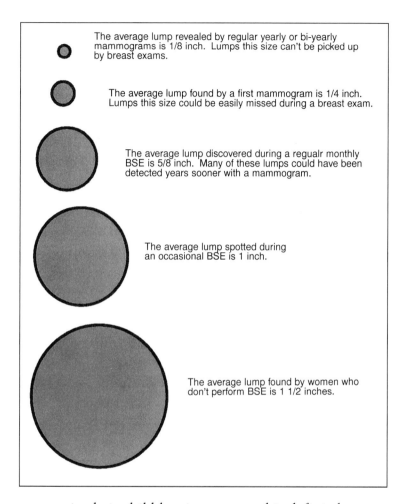

The average lump revealed by regular yearly or bi-yearly mammograms is 1/8 inch. Lumps this size can't be picked up by breast exams.

The average lump found by a first mammogram is 1/4 inch. Lumps this size could be easily missed during a breast exam.

The average lump discovered during a regualr monthly BSE is 5/8 inch. Many of these lumps could have been detected years sooner with a mammogram.

The average lump spotted during an occasional BSE is 1 inch.

The average lump found by women who don't perform BSE is 1 1/2 inches.

women in their child-bearing years and is definitely not a disease. It's a perfectly normal state!

Does breast-feeding prevent cancer?

Some experts believe nursing produces little or no effect on cancer-prevention. Others think it may lower risk a small amount by preventing ovulation. According to the latter belief, the longer breast-feeding continues the greater the benefit.

What is breast-cancer risk analysis and who should have it?

Many women with a family history of breast cancer feel certain that they will get it, too. Some see it as an ominous shadow stalking them and they set up their lives waiting for it to strike. Their overwhelming fear influences decisions about college, marriage, where to live, and even whether to have children.

Breast-cancer risk analysis may help them deal with their fears. It is a combination of genetic counseling, medical detective work, and a look at the statistics. When you reach adulthood, you may consider this option.

Will I Get Breast Cancer?

Vogel, Carole

Chapter Five:
Diagnosis and Treatment

Finding a suspicious breast lump can be frightening for any woman. She may want to wish it away and pretend it doesn't exist. But she needs to find out what it is—and soon. Her next step is to consult a physician who has experience with breast cancer.

If the doctor needs a better "look" at the lump, a mammogram may be ordered. [Mammograms are discussed in Chapter 4.] Sometimes physicians will check lumps in younger women with ultrasound instead of mammograms because the dense breast tissue of younger women renders mammograms almost useless. Ultrasound is also used with older women.

What is ultrasound?

Ultrasound is a device that transmits high-frequency sound waves through body tissues. When the sound waves

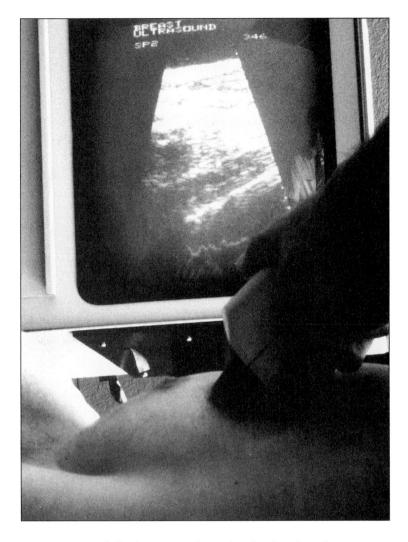

encounter solid objects within the body, they bounce or echo back. You can't hear, feel, or see the sound waves but the ultrasound device can detect them. It records the pattern of the echoes and transforms the recordings into a photographic image on a display screen. If nothing blocks their path, the sound waves pass through the body.

Ultrasound is a painless procedure and doesn't use X-rays. To allow the ultrasound transmitter/recorder to glide easily over the breast, the breast is covered with a film of jelly.

Ultrasound isn't a good screening tool—it can't consistently pick up breast lumps less than two centimeters and it can be confused by normal breast lumpiness. But ultrasound can determine whether lumps detected by other means are solid or fluid-filled. The sound waves pass through fluid-filled cysts and bounce off solid ones.

Ultrasound image of a breast lump

What is MRI?

Magnetic Resonance Imaging—MRI for short—is another tool that can provide a picture of the inside of the breast. It makes use of the magnetic properties of hydrogen atoms. The way it works is easy to understand. You probably know that your body is part water. You may also know that water molecules consist of two hydrogen atoms and one oxygen atom. But did you know that the nucleus of a hydrogen atom can act like a tiny magnet?

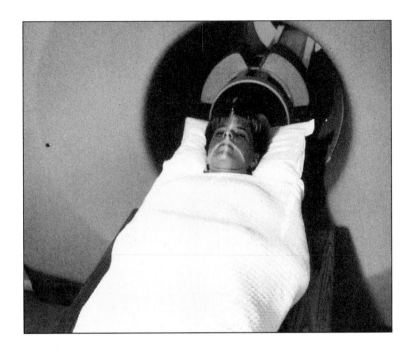

The MRI scanner is a huge magnet. It can magnetize the body's hydrogen atoms in the same way you can magnetize a paper clip with a magnet. The patient is placed in a cylinder that contains a powerful magnet. When the magnet is switched on, it creates a magnetic field. The nuclei of the hydrogen atoms line up in one direction. Then another magnetic field is turned on at right angles to the first. The nuclei begin to spin. While the nuclei spin, they send out signals. A computer records and translates the signals into a picture. When the magnet is switched off, the nuclei return to normal. Normal cells hold water more tightly than cancer cells so the difference between the two can easily be distinguished in an MRI scan. In fact, an MRI scan can reveal a cluster of cancer cells as tiny as three millimeters. The high cost of MRI scans prohibits their every-day use as a screening tool for breast cancer. In addition, it is a new test and its accuracy rate is still not known.

MRI of a breast

Are doctors always right?

Doctors can usually tell by examining a lump whether it should be investigated further. However, once in a very great while a physician can make a mistake. If you find a lump and your doctor dismisses your concerns, you most likely have absolutely nothing to worry about. But listen to your inner voice. You may want to consult with another doctor who has experience with breast cancer.

What is a biopsy?

If someone you know has breast cancer, her diagnosis was determined by a *biopsy* and microscopic examination of the tumor cells. In a biopsy a surgeon removes cells or tissue from a suspicious lump in one of four ways:

Type of Biopsy	How It's Done
Fine-needle biopsy	The surgeon inserts a small needle into the lump and removes a few cells. If fluid can be extracted, the lump can easily be identified as a harmless, fluid-filled cyst.
Core-needle biopsy	A special needle is used to cut out a small section from the lump.
Incisional biopsy	The surgeon makes a cut or *incision* in the skin and removes a large piece of the lump. This procedure is usually performed on large masses.
Excisional biopsy	The entire lump is completely removed. Surgeons perform these when lumps are small and easy to take out.

Most biopsies require local or general anesthesia for comfort. Local anesthesia numbs only the part of the breast with the lump. General anesthesia puts the patient to sleep. A fine-needle biopsy may be done with local anesthesia or none at all.

After the tissue is removed, it is sent to a pathologist, a physician who studies cells to determine disease. To check for cancer, the pathologist examines the tissue under a microscope. *About eighty percent of the time the findings show that the lump is harmless.* This means that most women who undergo biopsies learn they are cancer free! Many biopsies are done "just to be sure" on lumps that physicians think are probably harmless.

If a *malignancy* (cancer) is confirmed, the pathologist determines the kind of cancer present. [A discussion of the different kinds of breast cancer appears on pages 44-50.] The pathologist will also try to establish how quickly the cells divide and if the cancer has entered blood vessels or lymph vessels. The cells will be tested to find out whether hormones affect their growth. In general, tumors that react to hormones grow more slowly than tumors that don't react.

Biopsies alone cannot give a complete picture of how a cancer acts in a particular woman's body. Additional tests to determine *staging* are performed to learn whether the cancer has spread.

What is staging?

Cancer specialists devised a system called *staging* to describe how far a breast cancer has spread. Physicians use

Fine-needle biopsy

staging to make a prediction about a patient's future health
and determine which treatments are best.

What tests are used to determine staging?

One of the first steps in staging a tumor is to check the
lymph nodes for cancer cells. During the operation to
remove the breast tumor, lymph nodes beneath the arms
are surgically removed and sent to the pathologist.

STAGE	TUMOR SIZE	SIGNS OF SPREAD	MOST LIKELY OUTCOME
Carcinoma *in situ*	Very early breast cancer. Cancer cells found in a few layers in one spot.	It has not spread to nearby tissues.	It can nearly always be treated successfully by surgery alone or surgery and radiation. There is a 95 to 99 percent chance of long-term survival.
	Cancer cells are contained in the lining of the milk ducts and can occupy a large section of the breast.	Cancer cells have not spread outside the ducts.	"
Stage 1	Tumor is 2 cm (3/4 of an inch) or smaller.	Lymph nodes under the arm have no cancer. The cancer has not spread beyond the breast.	Excellent chance for long-term survival.
Stage 2	Tumor is between 2 and 5 cm (about 1-2 inches).	It may—or may not—have spread to the lymph nodes under the arm. No evidence of spreading has been found in distant parts of the body.	Usually responds well to treatment. Prognosis is usually good.
	Tumor is less than 2 cm.	Some of the lymph nodes contain cancer.	"
Stage 3	Tumor is larger than 5 cm (2 inches).	No signs of cancer have been detected in distant body parts.	The cancer is more advanced but sometimes Stage 3 tumors respond well to aggressive treatment.
	Tumor can be any size and has invaded the chest wall.	"	"
	The tumor can be any size and the cancer has spread to lymph nodes under the arm. The nodes have become stuck to the chest wall under the arm.	"	"
	The tumor can be any size and has spread to lymph nodes above the collar bone.	"	"
Stage 4	Tumor can be any size.	Cancer has spread to other parts of the body.	These cancers are usually not curable but often they can be slowed with treatment.

Underarm lymph nodes filter lymph that flows through the breast. They are one of the first places that breast cancer goes. If the lymph nodes contain cancer cells, there is a chance the cancer has spread to distant sites. [See page 46 for more about lymph and lymph nodes.]

When breast-cancer cells spread, they tend to wind up in the lungs, liver, bones, or skin. They may eventually metastasize to the brain. A chest X-ray can reveal if the cancer has spread to the lungs. A blood test can pick up unusual changes in the liver. A bone scan can detect areas of active tumor growth in the bones and a CAT-scan can uncover liver, lung, and brain tumors.

What is a bone scan?

You are probably familiar with how X-rays and blood tests are performed. A bone scan is a little more complicated. A very small dose of a *radioactive chemical* is injected into the patient's bloodstream. The chemical gives off invisible radiation. Your eyes can't see the radiation but special scanners can detect it.

The patient waits several hours for the chemical to be absorbed by her bone cells. Then she is scanned by a machine that counts the number of radioactive particles in her bones. It makes a picture of her skeleton that shows where the cells are most active. If the scan picks up a cluster of activity, X-rays of the area can reveal whether it is caused by cancer or not. The radiation used in this chemical is very short-lived and is eliminated in the urine within five to six hours.

How does a CAT-scan work?

The "CAT" in CAT-scan is short for *computerized axial tomography*. This device combines X-rays and computer technology to make detailed pictures of the body's soft tissues and internal organs. It can be used to check for liver and brain tumors and is often used to obtain a more detailed image of the lungs when a chest X-ray shows an abnormal finding. A CAT-scan can detect tiny tumors only two to three millimeters in size!

To make a CAT-scan, the patient lies on a table inside a donut-shaped machine. The CAT-scanner moves around the patient, sending narrow X-ray-beams through the body at different angles. A detector in the machine picks up the information revealed by the X-rays. A computer then translates the information into a series of cross-sections. The resulting pictures look like "slices" of the patient's body. CAT-scans provide a better image than plain X-rays but they also expose the body to more radiation.

Can the information taken from the biopsy, blood tests, X-rays, bone scan, MRI, and CAT-scan prove that the cancer has not spread?

All these tests can *confirm* the spread of cancer by revealing a mass of cancer. But they cannot prove that the cancer has *not* spread. They lack the ability to find individual stray cancer cells. So far, no method exists to establish conclusively that cancer cells have not metastasized. That's why regular checkups are important for breast-cancer patients.

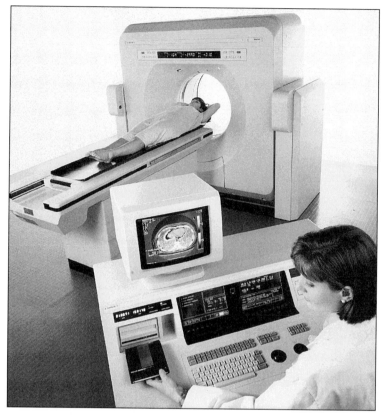

A CAT-scanner

What are the treatment options for breast cancer?

After cancer has been confirmed, the doctor and patient agree upon a plan of treatment. This plan is called a *protocol*. It depends mainly on the stage of the cancer. At the time this book was written, four main kinds of treatments existed: surgery, radiation therapy, chemotherapy, and hormone therapy. These options will be explained shortly. Perhaps by the time you read this, new and better treatments will be available.

Where can a woman find a second opinion?

Before beginning breast-cancer treatment, many women seek out a second cancer specialist to review their diagnosis and treatment plan. There are several different ways to get a second opinion:

- A woman's doctor may recommend another specialist.
- A woman can ask her doctor to discuss her case with another physician.
- Or, she may consult directly with another physician herself.
- To find the name of another specialist, a woman can ask friends for referrals or check with her hospital or local medical society.

What is a mastectomy and how does it differ from a lumpectomy?

A *mastectomy* is the surgical removal of the entire breast. For more than 70 years, the standard treatment for breast cancer was a *radical mastectomy*. In this operation the surgeon removed the entire breast, the chest muscles beneath the breast, and all the underarm lymph nodes. It left a woman with a hollow in her chest and a blow to her self-image.

The rationale for the radical mastectomy was that breast cancer advanced in a predictable order. Supposedly, it began in the breast, spread to the lymph nodes under the arms, and then traveled to other parts of the body. The radical mastectomy was intended to stop its progress.

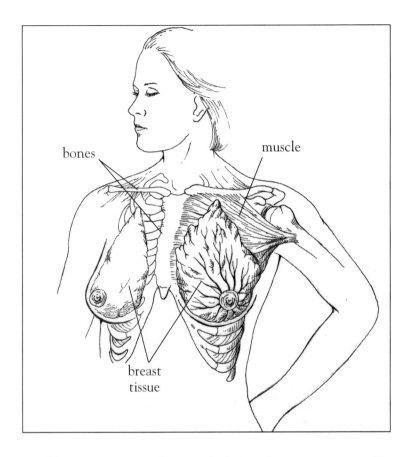

bones

muscle

breast
tissue

However, research revealed that breast-cancer cells start to roam early. They break off from the tumor and are whisked by the blood or lymph to distant organs. In the 1970s, less drastic surgery began to replace the radical mastectomy. The emphasis in treatment shifted to saving as much of the breast and surrounding tissue as possible while controlling the spread of cancer with radiation and chemotherapy.

To make sure no cancer cells remain in the breast after a lumpectomy or segmental mastectomy, women usually undergo radiation treatment. Studies show that lumpec-tomies followed by radiation treatment are just as effec-tive as mastectomies when the tumors are small.

Breast-Cancer Treatment

If someone you know was diagnosed with breast cancer she probably had one of these newer options for breast-cancer surgery:

• *Modified radical mastectomy*. The surgeon removes the breast, the lining of the chest muscles, and some or all of the underarm lymph nodes. The surgery does not leave a hollow in the chest.

• *Simple mastectomy*. This is similar to the modi-fied radical but usually no lymph nodes are removed.

• *Segmental mastectomy*. The surgeon takes out the section of the breast with the tumor, some skin above it, and the lining of the chest muscle below it. This procedure allows a woman to keep her breast. Through a separate incision, a few lymph nodes from under the arm are removed so they can be checked for the presence of cancer cells.

• *Lumpectomy*. This is another procedure that enables a woman to keep her breast. The surgeon removes the cancerous lump along with the rim of normal tissues surrounding it. The extra tissue is taken to ensure the complete removal of all cancer cells. Some lymph nodes are also taken through a separate incision so they can be checked.

Does the loss of underarm lymph nodes and lymph ves-sels cause lasting problems?

The loss of underarm lymph nodes and their connect-ing vessels may slow lymph circulation in the affected arm. As a result, the arm may swell. However, with today's sur-gical and radiation techniques, this is uncommon. Women with mastectomies must protect the affected arm from injury for the rest of their lives to reduce the risk of swelling. Swollen tissue is more prone to infection. Women with lumpectomies who had lymph nodes removed must also be careful.

Is surgery used to treat widespread cancer?

Sometimes tumors press against nerves, organs, or bones, creating pain or even blocking a vital function. Removing the tumor will make the patient feel better but unfortunately will not cure the cancer.

What is radiation therapy?

Radiation therapy begins three to seven weeks after cancer surgery. It uses high-powered, invisible rays from an X-ray machine to damage cancer cells and prevent them from reproducing. Radiation therapy is an effective weapon but it acts only in the area receiving the radiation. It isn't used to treat the whole body because it can hurt healthy cells, too.

Radiation therapy works best against small cancer growths in the breast. It may also be used to treat advanced breast cancer in other parts of the body. By shrinking large tumors, radiation therapy eases pain.

Radiation therapy creates some unpleasant side effects. However, if your mom or someone else you care for is going through this treatment (or had it in the past), you may be familiar with the side effects. The skin may become "sunburned" and a rash may appear. The patient

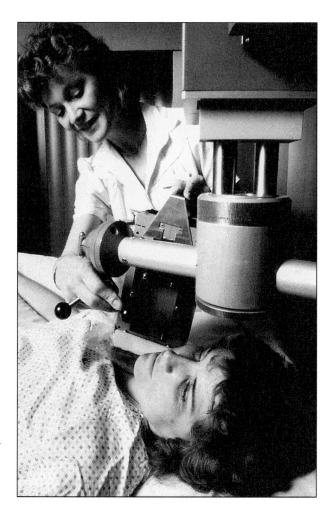

Radiation therapy

may feel tired—as though she has spent the day sun-bathing at the beach. These side effects disappear when the treatments are finished. Most women have little trouble with radiation therapy and can work full time and participate in most of their usual activities on the days they receive treatment. The most difficult aspect of radiation therapy may be the time involved. The patient must go for treatment five days a week for six weeks.

What is chemotherapy?

Chemotherapy is a treatment that uses powerful drugs to fight any cancer cells remaining in the body. These drugs can be taken by pill, injection, or IV. The drugs circulate in the bloodstream to places where the cancer cells may be hiding.

Anti-cancer drugs act in one or more of the following ways. They

- sabotage cell growth
- block cell division
- interfere with the cell's nutrition uptake and "starve" the cell to death.

As a cancer evolves, some of its cells may mutate again and again. As a result, tumors often contain different kinds of cancer cells. A drug that works against one type may be ineffective against the others. A combination of anti-cancer drugs provides the best treatment. Where one drug fails, another drug may succeed.

Unfortunately, anti-cancer drugs aren't choosy. They destroy some healthy, rapidly-growing cells, too. That's

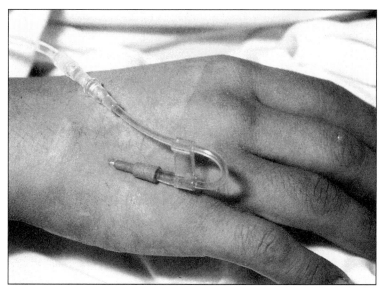

Medicine given by IV drips from a container into a tube. The tube connects to a needle that empties into a vein.

why they may cause side effects such as hair loss, nausea and vomiting, fever, loss of appetite, diarrhea, mouth sores, inflamed eyes, tiredness, and a flu-like feeling. The side effects depend on the type of drug, and vary from patient to patient. Not every patient becomes violently ill. But for those who do, special medication may ease their discomfort. Many anti-nausea drugs are available which are quite effective.

Chemotherapy frequently affects *bone marrow*, the innermost part of bone where blood cells develop. During treatment, fewer red blood cells, platelets, and white blood cells will form. As a result a patient may be pale and exhausted. She may bruise or bleed more easily. She will also be more prone to serious infection.

Patients who undergo chemotherapy may be embarrassed about their appearance, especially if they lose their hair temporarily. They may want to avoid visitors even though they need the encouragement of family and friends. If your mom is getting chemotherapy and feels this way, try to accept her appearance. Look her in the eye and try to see the person you love, not the changes. This may help her feel more comfortable. If she hasn't done so already, you might encourage her to wear a stylish wig, turban, or scarf. Chapter Six will give you other hints for dealing with your mom if she is undergoing cancer treatment.

Typically, chemotherapy is given over a period of six months, although four months may be enough. During this time the patient's *oncologist*—a doctor who specializes in cancer treatment—will watch her carefully. The oncologist wants to make sure the cancer drugs don't inflict any permanent damage. Many women can keep up with their usual activities during the course of chemotherapy treatments and side effects usually disappear when treatment ends. The nausea stops, hair grows back, and bone marrow returns to normal. The patient feels better and acts more like her old self.

With such nasty side effects, why is chemotherapy given?

To put it simply, the payoff makes it worthwhile. Chemotherapy prolongs life and often decreases the chance of the cancer returning. Chemotherapy probably fails to kill every stray tumor cell, but it may reduce the cancer to a level that the patient's immune system can handle. The role of the immune system will be discussed in Chapter Eight.

Why doesn't chemotherapy cure all cancer?

Some cancer cells may be *resistant* to the chemotherapy. The anti-cancer drugs will not destroy them. Premenopausal women—women who still menstruate—usually respond better to chemotherapy than postmenopausal women. However, post-menopausal women usually have a better response to hormone therapy.

How does hormone therapy work?

Almost two-thirds of all breast cancers require the hormone *estrogen* to grow. On the surface of these cancer cells lie structures called *receptors* which control the entry of estrogen. Various treatments exist to cut off the cell's access to estrogen. The most common treament is the drug *tamoxifen*.

Tamoxifen jams the receptors and keeps the cells from acquiring the estrogen they need. Its effectiveness as a cancer-preventing drug is currently being tested. Although it is taken mainly by older women who have stopped menstruating, it is also being tried on younger women. Tamoxifen produces some side effects but they are much less severe than those caused by chemotherapy. However, a few tamoxifen users have developed endometrial cancer. (The *endometrium* is the membrane that lines the uterus.)

Preventive surgery—the removal of the ovaries—eliminates the major source of female hormones in the body and starves tumor cells of estrogen. In the past it was the only option for younger women with advanced cancer. Now younger women can be treated with tamoxifen or chemotherapy. Chemotherapy causes many women to enter menopause early.

What is breast reconstruction?

To replace their missing breast, many women undergo surgery to construct a new one. Often, this surgery is performed during the same operation as a mastectomy. Some patients wait six months or more after a mastectomy to complete radiation or chemotherapy treatments before reconstruction. Not all women choose reconstructive surgery, which carries its own set of risks.

Several options exist for breast reconstruction:

- *Implant placement.* A sack filled with a saline solution—salt and water—is placed under the chest muscle. In the past, implants filled with silicone gel were commonly used. The government restricted their use after there was concern about health problems attributed to leaking implants. Saline implants may leak, too, but their contents are harmless and will be absorbed by the body. Of course, a leaky implant will need to be replaced as it will flatten like a deflated balloon. Researchers are looking into other kinds of materials to use in implants that are as safe as saline but won't leak as much.

- *Tissue transfer from the back.* A back muscle is used as a replacement for the breast tissue removed. An implant is placed beneath the muscle. Fat and skin from the back cover the muscle.

- *Tissue transfer from the abdomen.* One muscle from the abdomen is transplanted to the chest along with fat and skin. They are positioned to take on the shape of a breast.

- *Microsurgery.* In a delicate surgery, tissue covering the abdomen or buttocks is used to create a new breast.

A new areola and nipple can usually be created from skin on the upper thigh.

Although a reconstructed breast looks like a breast, it lacks the sensations of one. If it is stroked the woman doesn't feel the touch in the way she once did. The new breast also lacks milk glands so it cannot nurse a baby. But it helps a woman look more like her old self in and out of clothes. It also has the softness of her original breast.

Is reconstruction necessary?

No! Some women with mastectomies choose not to have reconstructive surgery. Many of them opt to wear the ultimate "falsie"—a *prosthesis.* Like breasts, prostheses come in many shapes and sizes. Women can buy special bras to hold the prosthesis or they can sew a pocket into a regular bra or bathing suit to accommodate it. In 1990, a new prosthesis was introduced that better mimics the weight and feel of a breast. It uses an adhesive to stick to

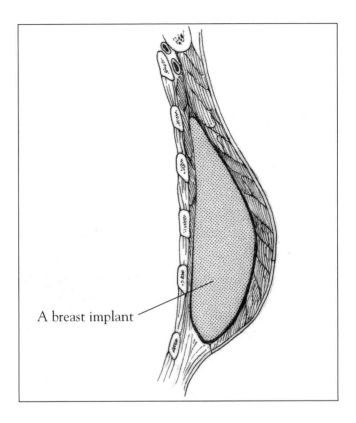

A breast implant

the chest so it doesn't slip. But, the adhesive can cause skin irritation so it's not right for everyone.

Some small-breasted women never bother with a prosthesis. When dressed there is little difference in their appearance and they are satisfied with the way they look. Others shun prostheses because they find them to be uncomfortable.

Some women feel no need to hide the fact of their surgery. They successfully ignore the pressure to conform to society's expectations of what is "womanly." For these women, having the appearance of two breasts is not vital to their self-esteem and they have no desire to hide their breast-cancer experience. However, there are drawbacks to this option. It's like wearing a sign that announces they have a history of breast cancer. When these women meet new people, their medical status comes immediately into focus and other qualities become secondary.

A few women have used their mastectomy scars to make a political statement about breast cancer. Matuschka, an artist who lost her right breast to cancer, uses nude self-portraits to shock. Her art forces people to confront the devastating impact of breast cancer. She, and other activists, want the U.S. Government to pour more money into much-needed breast-cancer research.

The choice to undergo reconstructive surgery, wear a prosthesis, or do nothing is highly personal and up to each individual woman. There is no right or wrong.

Can a woman who has had breast cancer still have sex?

Nothing prevents a woman who has had breast cancer from having a fulfilling sex life. A loving relationship builds on trust, common interests, shared experiences, as well as mutual attraction. Having sex will not make the cancer come back or spread faster. Her partner cannot catch cancer by touching, kissing, or sucking a breast.

After losing a breast some women have difficulty with intimacy because they don't feel good about themselves. They need time to regain their self-worth and learn they can still be beautiful without a breast. A supportive partner can be vital in a woman's adjustment to her new status.

Can a woman who has had breast cancer still have children?

Deciding to have children is a difficult choice for young women who have had breast cancer. They worry that they will not live long enough to raise their children. They wonder whether pregnancy hormones will make the cancer reappear.

No one can predict how pregnancy will affect any individual patient. Women who become pregnant after breast-cancer treatment seem to have the same chance of long-term survival as women who don't. This means some of these new mothers will live to see their children grow up, but sadly, others will not.

So how does a woman choose? She needs to consider her diagnosis and prognosis. Pregnancy hormones cannot cause cancer to spread but they may fuel the growth of stray cancer cells that are hormone sensitive. A woman whose lymph nodes contained cancer must decide if giving birth is worth the risk. But a woman whose cancer was found very early has an excellent chance of seeing her children grow and have children of their own.

Can a woman who had breast cancer nurse a baby?

The healthy breast will still produce milk in a woman with a history of breast cancer. If the woman underwent radiation treatment following a lumpectomy or segmental mastectomy, she will be unable to nurse in the affected breast. Radiation treatment damages milk-producing tissue.

Can a pregnant woman develop breast cancer?

A very small percentage of breast cancers occur in pregnant women. These cancers are difficult to detect because breasts thicken and become lumpier during pregnancy. Most lumps that arise in pregnancy are harmless. In rare cases they can mask a cancerous change and delay diagnosis and treatment. Women should examine their breasts monthly while pregnant and discuss any unusual finding with their health-care providers.

If a suspicious lump turns up, an ultrasound and biopsy can be performed with little risk to the fetus. However, treatment depends on the stage of the pregnancy. If the cancer is found during the first three months of pregnancy it will be difficult to battle the cancer and continue the pregnancy. The very treatments needed to save the life of the mother can hurt the fetus.

General anesthesia poses a slight risk of injury to the fetus but mastectomy is the treatment of choice for women who choose to keep the baby. Radiation and chemotherapy can harm the fetus. If a young woman in the early months of pregnancy clearly needs chemotherapy she will usually be advised to terminate the pregnancy so she can undergo treatment. However, the difficult choice to end the pregnancy or not is always her own to make.

If a cancer is found in the middle and later months of pregnancy general anesthesia can be used with less risk to the fetus. A mastectomy can be performed. The use of radiation and chemotherapy treatments, however, can still be hazardous to the fetus and cannot be given any time during the pregnancy.

Sometimes it is safe to perform surgery during the pregnancy and delay other treatments until after the child is born. The cancer itself poses no threat to the baby. Breast-cancer cells cannot spread to it. To treat the mother sooner, the baby may be delivered early by caesarean section when it is able to live on its own.

Does breast cancer occur in nursing mothers?

Nursing mothers can develop breast cancer but it doesn't happen very often. The changes due to breast feeding make the disease hard to detect. If a nursing mother finds an unusual and persistent lump, her physician should check it out. If a biopsy reveals breast cancer, the baby can be switched to bottle feeding and treatment can begin immediately. Incidentally, the mother *cannot* pass cancer to the baby through her milk.

What is remission?

Breast cancer that spreads to distant parts of the body can rarely be cured, but it can seem to disappear. This *remission* can last for months or years before the cancer flares up again. The longer a cancer stays in remission before reappearing, the more treatable it will be. Many women who have had breast cancer live to an old age and die of other causes.

What happens if breast cancer reappears?

If breast cancer comes back, the treatment will depend on

- the location of the cancer
- whether it's widespread
- if the patient still menstruates or not
- the patient's overall health
- how the patient reacted to the initial therapy

If the disease returns to the same breast after a lumpectomy and radiation treatment, a mastectomy and possibly a *systemic* treatment, such as chemotherapy or hormone therapy will be recommended. Surgery, radiation, and systemic therapy may all be recommended if the recurrence occurs on the chest wall after a mastectomy.

Breast cancer rarely spreads from one breast to the other. If it develops in the unaffected breast, it will be treated like a new cancer. If the cancer turns up in other parts of the body, chemotherapy and hormone therapy may be prescribed. In this case, surgery and radiation therapy may also be implemented to slow its progress and relieve pain.

Can breast cancer be cured?

Fortunately, breast cancer can be cured when it is caught early. But women with advanced cancer should not abandon hope. Medical researchers continually seek more effective treatments for early and advanced cancers. The lives of breast-cancer patients are being extended with new approaches to treatment. Chapter Eight describes current research that may lead to a cure in the future.

Chapter Six:
Coping When a Mother Has Breast Cancer

If your mother had breast cancer, do you remember how you felt when you first learned about it? If you were old enough to understand the serious nature of the disease you probably felt numb or shocked. You couldn't believe what was happening. Perhaps a zillion thoughts seemed to swirl in your brain and you couldn't focus on a single one. Or maybe your mind just seemed to shut down completely.

After the news sank in you may have wondered, *Why her? Why my mother? Who will take care of me?* Suddenly, your life had changed. Something terrible was happening and you had no control over it. Even worse your mother could not control events either. You felt like your life would never be normal again.

When cancer strikes, it affects the whole family. Everybody worries whether the patient will get better or not, but each individual may react differently. Family members may feel tense, angry, helpless, afraid, sad, confused, or lonely. Some may withdraw; others may talk nonstop. Some may become quarrelsome, while others may act as though nothing is wrong. You may even wonder if anybody else but you cares that your mother is sick.

If you don't understand why the people around you act the way they do, ask them—nicely. You cannot change the fact that your family is upset. But by talking things out you may be able to understand everybody's feelings—including yours—better.

Why am I so angry?

Adults are supposed to be in control! Moms especially aren't supposed to get sick—at least that's what most kids would like to believe. When your mother became ill, it may have felt like a betrayal. After all, it's the mom's responsibility to take care of the kids, right? Many households depend on the mom to do almost everything. They shop and prepare meals, take care of laundry and cleaning, run car pools, help with homework, and remind kids to eat right, brush their teeth, and pick up after themselves. It's normal to feel angry when you feel you have been let down.

Sometimes anger masks feelings of fear or helplessness. It may be easier to act angry and pick fights than to admit you feel scared or helpless.

You may also be upset because your family expects you to pick up your mother's slack. Suddenly, your mother's chores become your problem. You may be expected to help her out—bring her meals, get her water, fetch a book, answer the phone, watch younger siblings—little tasks that may add up to one big bother. Just when you are reaching the age when you want to spend more time with friends and become more independent, you are suddenly being sucked right back into the family. No wonder you're upset!

To make matters worse, you may begin to resent your mom and become impatient with her. You probably show it. You might even explode and yell at her. And then what happens? You feel guilty.

You are not alone. Many kids whose mothers have breast cancer or any other serious illness become angry at their mothers for getting sick and disrupting their lives. Some kids become upset because they think they are expected to do too much. Others are furious because they may have to live somewhere else while their mothers are in the hospital. Still others react to parents who themselves are acting angry, impatient, or unfair. Getting angry is a natural reaction. It doesn't mean you don't love your mom or that you are a terrible daughter.

How do I deal with my anger?

The first step in controlling anger is to become aware that it is building before you explode. If you feel yourself getting upset, ask yourself why. Are you hungry? Tired? Lonely? Frustrated? Scared? Feeling unappreciated? Reacting to someone else's anger? Could this be PMS? [Refer back to page 29 for more information on PMS.]

To avoid a blowup, call for a time out to cool down. Seek the solitude of your room or take a walk to collect your thoughts. Some people find exercise to be a constructive outlet. If you leave the house tell somebody where you are headed. You don't want to heap worry onto an already tense situation.

You can use *visualization* to soothe your anger. Picture a peaceful scene in your mind, perhaps a beach or mountaintop. Put yourself in the picture and walk around. What do you see, hear, touch, smell? Continue to explore until you feel calm again. Prayer or meditation may also help you find peace of mind.

If you use anger to protect yourself from feeling sad, fearful, helpless, guilty, or from other troubling emotions, you need to let out these feelings. The best way is to find someone with whom you can talk. This is especially true if you are frightened that your mother's fate will be your own. Speak with your father or choose a friend who will listen and respect your confidences by not sharing your worries with others.

How can I regain control over my life?

Learn how to solve problems constructively. If something is bothering you, identify the problem and write it down. Then list several of your options. Next to each one note its good and bad points. After weighing your options, draw up a plan of action. Set a deadline to put the plan into place and then DO IT!

How can I reduce stress?

Keeping healthy and fit is a key to reducing stress. If you eat properly and get enough sleep you will be better equipped to handle difficult situations. Exercise at least twenty minutes a day, three to seven times a week, to work out tension, anger, and depression. You needn't do anything elaborate—a brisk walk or a bike ride is often enough.

Who can I talk to?

It's hard to constantly put up a brave front all by yourself. You need to find one or more people to help you through this difficult time. Finding someone to listen to you and support you may feel scary in itself, especially if in the past you confided your big worries to your mom.

Try your father first but if this is not possible, make a list of people you respect. This list may include grandparents, aunts, uncles, cousins, teachers, neighbors, friends of your parents, parents of your friends, a rabbi, minister, or priest, guidance counselor, school nurse, scout leader, coach, older sibling, friends, or a former babysitter.

Choose one or more people who seem to be good listeners and who you think will answer questions honestly. Then telephone or visit them. If you're not sure what to say, you can always start out with news about your mom. You can then gauge from the response whether you will feel comfortable confiding in the person or not. You will find that some people know just what to say and are sensitive to your feelings. Others have no understanding of what you are going through and you may feel worse. Keep looking until you find someone with whom you feel comfortable.

A support group made up of other sons and daughters of cancer patients can provide an excellent source of strength and comfort. These groups provide a safe setting for kids to talk about their worries and share their experiences. Many hospitals provide support groups for families of cancer patients. If your mother's hospital does not offer such a service, the American Cancer Society can tell you where to find a support group. Their toll free number is 1-800-227-2345.

Sometimes belonging to a support group or sharing feelings with someone you trust is not enough. If you have extra problems or concerns that you can't work out, a social worker, psychologist, nurse therapist, or family therapist may be your best bet for help. The nurses or doctors at your mother's hospital should be able to help you find a good one.

Why are some of my friends dropping me?

When your mom was first diagnosed with cancer most of your friends probably felt sorry for you but now some of them may be leaving you alone. This happens to lots of kids in your situation.

Some friends may not know what to say or do around you. Others may feel embarrassed or uneasy when they visit your home and see your mother looking ill. Her appearance may scare them or they may mistakenly think they can pick up cancer germs!

You could be acting a little weird, too, because of the stress you are feeling. Your friends may think you don't want to spend time with them anymore. Hard as it may seem, the only thing you can do is reach out to your friends and explain how you feel. You may need to tell them *how* to be your friend right now.

If you lose friends, you will be able to make new ones. Perhaps you know someone in school who has already had experience with a very sick parent. That person probably understands what you are going through now.

Your mother may also be having difficulties with her friends. She may be disappointed if they don't make the effort to "be there" for her while she is ill. Some of her friends may want to help but do not know how to offer. Others might be "fair-weather friends"—people who can share good times but lack the maturity to help out in the bad. They may be reluctant to visit a sick person because they are afraid to think about illness and death.

Nobody tells me anything—how do I find out what's going on?

Some parents are too wrapped up with their own concerns to tell their kids what is happening. Others try to protect their children by withholding information. They may think the truth might be too painful or that the child is not old enough to handle it.

Not knowing, however, can be worse than anything. If

you feel left out, make a list of questions that you need to have answered. Go over the list with your parents if you can. If this is not possible, ask another adult whom you trust. If your mother's doctor or nurses seem friendly you might approach them for answers.

Try to learn all you can about breast cancer. One good way is to read books about it but make sure the information is current. Check the copyright date on the inside of the book. If it is more than a few years old, some of the cancer information may be out-of-date.

For more current information, try these women's magazines: *Glamour, Ladies' Home Journal, Redbook, McCall's, Vogue,* and *Good Housekeeping.* They do a good job of reporting on breast cancer. Their up-to-date articles are written in a clear, easy-to-understand style. To identify recent back issues which will be useful, look under "breast cancer" in your library's *Reader's Guide to Periodical Literature, Infotrac,* or *Magazine-Article Summaries.* If you need help using any of these indexes or finding the articles, ask your librarian. While you are in the library, find out if they stock any videos about breast cancer, too.

If you still have questions, you can call the National Cancer Institute Information Service. Their information specialists can answer questions and send you additional information. Their toll-free number is 1-800-422-6237. Volunteers at the American Cancer Society can provide information, too. Again, their toll free number is 1-800-227-2345.

What is happening to my mother emotionally?

Your mother is being hit with a double whammy. Having cancer forces her to confront her own mortality, no matter how good her prognosis. Death stops being something that happens only to other people; she realizes that someday she will die. Even though more women survive breast cancer than ever before, virtually all women who receive a diagnosis of breast cancer feel for some period of time like they are staring death in the face.

Breast cancer also assaults your mother's sense of self, especially if a mastectomy was necessary. She is saying goodbye to the woman she thought she was and is confronting a new reality. For a while, she may not feel like she is a whole woman. She may wonder if she'll ever feel attractive or pretty again. As she copes with her sense of loss, she may feel like her body has betrayed her. She may feel all alone and believe that nobody in the whole world understands how she feels.

Your mother must also adjust to an invasion of her privacy. To battle cancer, she has to allow many different people to look at and touch her breasts. She may begin to feel as though she is less of a person as her medical team focuses on her breasts and fails to see her as a whole human being. Some members of the team may even begin to treat her like a child and this may diminish her self-esteem further.

Everything in your mother's life has changed. *She* has changed. She may be coping with fatigue, pain, arm swelling, hair loss, as well as the removal of a breast. This loss of control over her body and the disruption of her routine may make her feel helpless and frustrated. On top of this the cancer treatment may make her feel plain lousy or violently ill.

Your mother may be just as frightened and angry as you are. She might think she is letting her family down and worry about how *you* are coping. She is probably concerned that she passed a tendency for breast cancer on to you.

With all your mother has to work through, it should be no surprise if she acts cranky, sad, depressed, withdrawn, angry, tired, or totally involved with herself. Yet knowing why she behaves strangely doesn't make it easier for you if motherhood has sunk to the bottom of her priority list. This may be especially difficult if at times your mother doesn't want to talk to you or acts as though she doesn't care. Remember, despite all the changes, deep down your mother still loves you very much.

What is happening to my family?

Your mother's illness impacts on all the members of your family. Everybody is hurting, but each person expresses their pain in their own individual way. You may find it scary to see your parents cry or your siblings act out by becoming defiant, bossy, or belligerent.

Your father may be so focused on your mother's needs that he lacks the energy to meet yours, especially if he's shuttling back and forth to the hospital or clinic. You may rarely eat meals together as a family and nobody may be home to help with your homework, drive you to your friend's house, or provide a listening ear. As a result you may feel left out or neglected. Remember, your mother is the focus of attention because she needs it, not because you are less loved.

It would be wonderful if catastrophe brought out the best in every family member. But often the opposite occurs—people become more short-tempered and impatient with each other. Their worst traits may become exaggerated or they may retreat into themselves. To keep things in perspective, remember that your family had its ups and downs before your mother got cancer.

You are having a hard enough time sorting out your own feelings without having to figure out what is going on in everybody else's head. Yet you will have an easier time if you understand their thinking. Family meetings may soothe tempers by giving each person a chance to express their concerns. This is especially important if you or one of your siblings has become overly bossy or if you feel you are being nagged constantly one day and totally ignored the next. Keep in mind that not every argument is worth winning. It won't hurt you to give in every once in a while.

Sitting down together and reassigning responsibilities may help the household run with less friction. If money is a problem, brainstorm ways to spend less. Devise a "time-out" signal so people can cool down when tempers flare.

I feel like I am responsible for my mother's cancer. How can I stop feeling guilty?

In anger, did you ever tell your mom that you wished she were dead? Did she ever say, *You'll be the death of me,* or *You make me sick?* Conflicts between mothers and daughters are as natural as thunderstorms and rain. Your mom probably experienced the same kind of fights with her mother! Words may be powerful weapons in arguments but they don't cause cancer. **Nothing you said, did, or thought made your mother sick.** You don't have the power to give someone cancer.

If your mother or father pays less attention to you or snaps at you more often, you may mistakenly believe that you've done something terribly wrong. Their change in behavior reflects their worry and preoccupation with the cancer and how it has impacted on their lives. It is not your punishment for making your mother sick.

If I am super good will my mother get better?

You also don't have the power to heal your mother. Whether or not you are the perfect child will make no difference in your mother's fight against cancer. Being super good all the time will only add to your own stress. Just be yourself.

I can feel normal one moment and be crying the next. How can I control my mood swings?

Mood swings plague most teenagers because adolescents react intensely to inner and outer influences. Often they magnify problems way out of proportion to reality. It's common to be on top of the world one moment and down in the pits the next.

To control your mood swings better, put your feelings into words instead of acting out. Keep a journal or record your feelings on audio or videotape. Try to describe what you are feeling to a parent or a friend.

Some things are worth crying about. Being scared for your mother and worrying about yourself is reason enough. Perhaps you can find a safe time or place to release your tears without embarrassment.

Is it normal to feel sorry for myself?

It's okay to feel sorry for yourself. Since your mom got cancer, nothing in your life seems to be the same and your parents can't give you the time and the attention you need. But remember, you are not helpless. If you feel lonely, find someone with whom you can share your thoughts. If you believe too much responsibility has been shifted onto you, discuss this with your parents. If you imagine you are the only girl who has a mother with cancer, go to the library and find books about other kids who have dealt with similar situations.

But, remember when you read about other cancer patients and their families, don't assume that what happens to them will happen in your family. Each cancer patient and each family is unique.

Is it normal to cling to my mother? I am afraid something bad will happen if I am not there.

You cannot protect your mother from her cancer or from the side effects of treatment. Remember—more women are living with breast cancer and living longer than in the past. Researchers are working on new ways to treat cancer and prolong life.

Why do I laugh when my mother tries to talk to me about her cancer?

Some people handle emotionally-charged situations by laughing. Laughter may be your outlet for nervousness. Or, it may be your way of showing you are not yet ready to talk about cancer. Perhaps you are afraid of what your mother might tell you. Confront your fear by listing on paper the worst things she could say. Go over the list with your father or somebody else you trust. You might find you have been scaring yourself needlessly. Then find out what your mom needs to share.

What can I do to make hospital visits more pleasant?

Hospitals can be very unsettling places. The sounds, smell, equipment, constant bustle, and all the sick people—including your mom—provide continual reminders that life is fragile.

You might find some members of your mom's medical team to be welcoming and understanding. Others may not be kid-friendly at all. They might lack the skills and compassion to communicate with young people or they may be too rushed to take the time. If you encounter doctors or nurses who make you feel unwelcome or invisible, try not to take it personally. After all, you know what a great kid you are. Not getting to know you is their loss!

Make you mother's hospital room more pleasant by decorating it with photographs of family members and friends, artwork, and get-well cards. Give her a small tape player so you can listen to music together. You can make a tape recording of memories you share and give it to her.

These are activities you can do with your mom if she is feeling up to it.

- Tell her what is happening in your life.
- Read books aloud.
- Watch TV.
- Play card or board games.
- Record the family history.
- Write a story together and then record it on video or audiotape.
- Share a joke of the day. (Ask your librarian or book-seller to recommend good joke books.)
- Bring in a picnic meal so you can eat together.
- Consult about homework.
- Ask her for advice. (Moms usually love this!)

What is an appropriate homecoming for my mother?

A clean house or apartment is probably the best gift you can give your mom. There are few things as demoralizing as returning to a messy home when you are feeling lousy. The most important rooms to put in order are her bedroom, the living room, bathroom, and kitchen. If you don't know where things belong just stack them in *neat* piles. Be sure to wash all the dirty dishes (including pots), wipe the counters clean, and take out the garbage. If you are pressed for time, vacuum only the dirtiest rugs. If your room is a disaster area, simply keep the door closed until you have time to straighten it.

Leaving the hospital may be upsetting for your mom. In the hospital her medical team took care of her and assumed responsibility for her health. Now her well being is in her own hands and that may seem overwhelming. She may not appear to be overjoyed at first to be home.

How can I help my mother when she is at home?

To help your mom return to normal keep her involved in your life. Let her know what is happening in school and with your friends. Say goodbye before you leave the house and greet her when you return. If you need adult permission to do something like visit friends, be sure to ask her.

New restrictions may be placed on you while your mother recovers. For example, she may ask you to keep the volume low when you play music or watch TV. Or she may ask you not to have friends over while she is resting. You may resent these restrictions—what teenager wouldn't?—but sometimes your mother must come first.

Try to anticipate your mom's needs so she doesn't have

to constantly ask you to run errands. Bring her snacks, meals, cold or warm drinks, the newspaper, books to read, and so on. Help her write thank-you cards. If your family can afford a portable telephone, now is a great time to buy one if you don't own one already. You can bring the phone to her anywhere in the house.

If you feel comfortable cooking and cleaning up the mess afterward, either prepare your mom's favorite meals, or supplement packaged and takeout foods with a good, healthy salad. If someone else is looking after your mom and you aren't sure where you fit in, ask what you can do to help.

Once your mother starts her treatment program, try to establish a daily and weekly routine with your family. Make sure you understand your responsibilities. Try to be flexible! With so many unknowns in your life right now, your plans may fall through. Try to channel your disappointment constructively by making alternate arrangements.

How can I tell my mother I am being expected to do too much?

Helping out constantly can be wearing. It is normal to feel resentful of your mother for needing your help. But remember, she isn't deliberately acting helpless or lazy. Yelling at her will just make you both feel bad so try to curb your temper. In case you don't, apologize as soon as you have cooled down.

If you feel overburdened, calmly talk to your mother or your father and negotiate a way to relieve the pressure on you. Now is the time to take up the offers of help that friends and neighbors have made. Make a list of your duties that can be handed over to others—at least for a little while. If your parents can afford one, suggest that they hire a temporary homemaker or home health aide. You need to take breaks—visit friends, talk on the phone, veg out in front of the TV, or just get away for a short time.

Am I a selfish person if I forget about my mom for a while and have fun?

You are *not* a selfish person if you find the time and space for your own needs. Your mother knows it's important for you to have fun and be happy even though she may feel awful. You are entitled to moments of joy and laughter. These breaks will refresh you. Enjoying yourself does not mean you have stopped loving your mother. You need to find ways to have fun. Perhaps the whole family can brainstorm entertaining activities to participate in together. Taking care of yourself is a necessity!

I get into trouble at school and rebel at home. What is wrong with me?

You are at that time in life—adolescence—when children break away from their parents. Sometimes your need to be independent clashes with your parents' desire to control. You may question and criticize your parents' values and behaviors. You may resent their attempts to tell you what to do. Add to this already turbulent situation the stress of breast cancer and what happens?

You may fight more with your parents, siblings, and friends. You may get angry at your mom for being sick and then feel guilty about it. You may make a major production over a minor sniffle or a little pimple. Your class work may suffer. You may be more tired, grouchy, and disorganized than usual. If your mother helped with your homework and no one fills the gap, you may slip behind.

Some of what's going on, however, may not be simple adolescent rebellion. Some kids in your situation break rules at home and in school in a subconscious attempt to attract attention. They may be feeling the loss of their parents' attention and may even feel rejected. An angry reaction from a parent or teacher may seem better than no attention at all. Misbehaving may be your way of saying, *Don't forget about me!*

It may also be a way of gaining control. You know if you act outrageously you will evoke an angry response. Some kids find it comforting to test limits and provoke a negative response. They feel more secure knowing that at least some things never change.

Other kids make scenes as a diversion. By stirring up trouble they distract the family from worrying about the cancer. This behavior is actually self-defeating because it only creates more stress.

Still other kids regress—they slip into behaviors typical of younger children. This is their way of saying, *I feel like a little kid. I want someone to take care of me.*

Right now, life is hard for you. You feel different from your friends and you don't see an end to it. How you choose to respond to this situation can make a difference. You need to learn how to handle stress and live with worry for a long time. Getting in touch with your feelings and expressing them can help you adjust better.

Is it okay to keep my feelings inside?

Some kids bottle up their emotions because they want to put up a strong front. They don't want to upset their mother by crying in front of her, especially if the mother has struggled to maintain a strong front herself. Others keep their feelings inside because they are afraid of them. Yet, to cope, you need to express your sad feelings. It's okay to cry. And it's okay for the family to cry together, too.

You need to share feelings with someone. You've heard this before—but are you listening? The best gift you can give yourself now is to find someone to listen to you and support you.

After cancer treatment ends, will life return to normal?

Don't expect family life to return to normal the minute cancer treatment ends. Physically, your mom may still be weak and very tired. When she gets a burst of energy she may push herself too hard and become exhausted. For example, if the house became trashed while she was sick, she may want to tackle it immediately and she'll probably expect you to help. In the middle of cleaning she may become so tired she has to stop, but she'll expect you to finish the job! Do you see the potential for conflict here?

You may find your mother hard to live with as she learns her own limitations. She may be grouchier than usual and take out her impatience on the rest of the family. The most difficult adjustment may be adapting to new family roles. During your mother's illness you became more independent and made more decisions by yourself. Now your mother may want to return to the way it was but you may be unwilling to give up your newly-found freedom. Together you will need to work out new boundaries.

This need to become reacquainted with your mother may be quite upsetting, especially if you thought everything would be back to normal when she felt better. Adjusting to her recovery may be just as difficult as adjusting to her sickness! If the conflicts seem unresolvable, family therapy may provide solutions.

Believe it or not, as your mother's health improves you may discover that some good has come out of this whole experience.

- You may feel closer and more loving toward your parents and siblings.
- You might feel proud of your family's ability to cope under severe stress.
- You may have enhanced your appreciation for life and family.

- You might be more responsible and self-reliant.
- You may have become more understanding of the needs of others.
- You will be able to advise and comfort friends when bad times overwhelm their lives.
- You will have learned how to tackle difficult problems and find creative solutions for them.
- You will have gained the knowledge that you can face terrible situations and survive.

Will the cancer come back?

Breast cancer detected in the early stages can usually be cured, but more advanced cancers may reappear. The outcome can go either way and this can make the years following treatment very difficult emotionally.

Worrying about whether the cancer has spread is only natural. Every time your mother reports for a checkup you may feel particularly anxious. You may feel frustrated when you ask about the possibility of a recurrence and the response is *we don't know*. Often that is the truth—no one may be able to tell you definitely whether your mother has been cured.

Doctors are armed with these statistics that may or may not apply to your mother.

- Sixty percent of the breast cancers *that come back* appear within the first three years.
- Another twenty percent of returning cancers occur within four to five years.
- Twenty percent recur in later years.

Living with uncertainty is one of the most horrible aspects of breast cancer. Some girls grow up with the sense that they could suddenly find themselves without a mother. For most, the worry decreases over time. But keep in mind that even if the cancer returns, more women are living with breast cancer than ever before and new treatments are continually being found.

Chapter Seven:
Losing the Battle

This may be the most upsetting chapter of the book. It will not apply to you if your mother's cancer treatment has been successful. But sadly, some cancer treatments fail and cannot stop the spread of cancer.

If your mother is losing the battle to cancer, you may realize it deep inside even if no one has told you. You may have overheard a doctor's comment or something a friend or relative said. The information you gleaned from reading may have given you the clue. Or maybe you just plain know. If an adult hasn't confirmed your suspicions, ask. You have a right to know if your mother's illness is expected to result in death. Perhaps, you are wrong and you are terrifying yourself needlessly.

But what if you are correct? To help you through this very difficult time, you may want to read and discuss this chapter with your father, a friend, or another adult you trust.

How long will my mother live?

If the cancer spreads, no one can tell you for sure how long your mother will live. Doctors can give you statistical averages that may or may not apply to your mother. These numbers tell you what happened to other women *in the past*. Like an old photograph they provide a good historical record but don't reflect the present. They fail to account for recent advances in cancer treatment and your mother's own unique situation.

The only certainty you have is that things will continue to change. *You* will continue to change and grow, just as you have grown and changed since your mother's cancer was first detected. If your mother has been sick for a while you have already adjusted to living without her in many respects. You have become more independent.

Who will take care of me if my mother dies and I don't have a father?

This is a good question to discuss with your mother if possible. She may already have asked someone to be your guardian. If so, her wishes should be protected by spelling them out in a will. A will helps to ensure that everybody will understand your mother's instructions. Find out if your mother has also made provisions for your financial support and education plans. If your mother has not chosen a guardian, ask her to consider it. Tell her who you think could provide you with a secure and loving home.

If you can't talk about a guardian with your mother, make a list of all the people you and your mother love.

These people know you are not old enough yet to live alone and they would make sure you would be settled in a good home. It is scary but okay to think about life without your mother. *All* kids at some time or another fantasize about life without their parents.

Is it normal to withdraw from my mother and avoid her?

If your mother has been ill for a long time, her appearance may have changed so much that you find it hard to touch her and give her hugs. Perhaps she moans or makes other unusual sounds. Maybe she has developed an unpleasant smell. All of these changes may repulse you and make you feel guilty for feeling that way.

Remember that inside that body is the same woman you have always known and who wants you to know that she loves you. When you were small, she took you by the hand when you needed help climbing stairs or crossing streets. Now she needs your help. Try to take her hand and look her in the eye when you speak with her. Let your mother know you love her. Try not to think about how she looks.

Sometimes medication or illness can change someone's personality so much you almost don't recognize them. If your mother is constantly cranky, sleepy, forgetful, or distant, it can be very frightening. Try to identify a time of day to approach her when she seems to be more of her old self. The changes in your mother's personality may be unpredictable. On good days she may be friendly and concerned—much like the old mom you remember. On bad days she may answer you with silence and turn away.

If your mother has withdrawn completely from you, it's time to talk to your father or someone you trust about what is going on. You need to know what is causing the changes and if the changes will go away. Remember, the old mom would never, never stop loving you. It is just the illness or the drugs that makes her act the way she does.

What will happen if my mother is dying?

If your mother is dying you may worry about how comfortable she is able to be. Taking care of her may be too great a burden for your family, even with the help of a nurse or health-care aide. She may require assistance just to eat, bathe, or relieve herself, and she may need to receive pain-killers by injection or IV. If she cannot be cared for at home, a hospital, nursing home, or hospice may be the best possible place for her.

You may find yourself being incredibly angry with your mother for being so ill and then you may feel very guilty about being angry at her for dying. This is a very common experience. Anger and guilt, as well as sadness, often spread themselves around when somebody is in the process of dying. Even your mother may feel angry and guilty about being so helpless and about leaving you before you are fully grown.

You may find it very frightening if your father and other adults cry or act totally out of character. Simply because they are adults doesn't mean they can be in control all the time. Despite their good intentions, they may not know what to do or say in this situation to help you. After a period of mourning, when they have had a chance to reflect on your mother's life and death, they will find the strength to carry on. So will you. In the meantime, seek out other adults whom you trust.

What are the "stages of dying?"

During a terminal illness a patient *may* go through one or more of these five stages that were described by psychiatrist Dr. Elizabeth Kübler-Ross in her book, *On Death and Dying:*

1. *Shock and Denial*—The patient is unable to believe that she is dying.

2. *Anger*—When the truth sinks in, she becomes angry. She realizes she's going to lose all the people she loves, as well as herself. Her rage may be vented on the people closest to her.

3. *Bargaining*—The patient tries to make a deal, usually with God or herself, to forestall death. She might make a promise like, "I'll never lose my temper again if you let me live until next spring."

4. *Depression*—The patient gives into despair and grieves her own impending death.

5. *Acceptance*—Some dying people, but not all, make peace with themselves and with the world.

The dying person's family may also go through these stages. In addition, they may feel relieved when the patient dies because her suffering and their own ordeal have ended.

What will happen to me if my mother dies?

Even if you know death is inevitable, it is still an awful shock when it happens. You may find it hard to accept. For a while you may feel numb or you may hate your mother for dying and leaving you. Eventually you will feel the hurt of losing her. You'll wonder if life will ever be normal again. The pain will gradually lessen, but your love for your mother will stay. Life goes on and someday you will feel happy feelings again.

After losing a mother, you may worry that your father may also die too soon. The likelihood of both your parents dying while you are young is very, very slim. A good therapist can help you deal with your loss by giving you the chance to talk about your innermost feelings and concerns. Counseling may be especially helpful if you and your mother shared a stormy relationship or if your mother was mean to you at times. Your therapist or counselor can help you sort through the good and the bad memories so you can eventually come to terms with who your mother really was.

If you are adopted, you may have to deal with an extra issue. You may feel that you have been abandoned twice—first by your birth mother and then by your adopted mother. Counseling may help you come to terms with your losses and help you realize that you are not at fault.

Will my life ever be normal again?

Your life will become normal again but it will be a different normal, one without your mother. You will establish a new day-to-day routine.

Your mother will always be part of you. Throughout your life you will have reminders. When you are confused and in need of advice you may think of her. When you have good news you want to share, you may remember her. As you grow older you may see your mother's features when you glance at a mirror or gaze into your children's eyes. Many of these reminders will spark wonderful memories that leave you smiling. Others will leave you sad and teary-eyed.

Some experiences may be especially difficult.

- Mother's Day with all its commercial messages.
- Watching your friends interact with their moms.
- Listening to friends complain about their mothers.
- Bumping into your mother's friends or co-workers.
- Seeing other mother and daughter pairs doing the things you long to do with your mother.
- TV shows, movies, and plays that feature the mother-daughter relationship.
- Adjusting to a stepmother if your father remarries.

Losing your mother is probably one of the most terrible things that can happen to you. But the important thing to know is that your life *will* go on. You will continue to grow and develop into a young woman with an exciting life of your own. You still can fulfill your dreams and be a good mom yourself someday. The knowledge that you can survive just about anything will be carried with you for the rest of your life.

Chapter Eight:
What's in the Future?

Wouldn't it be great if cancer could be treated the way most medical problems are solved on *Star Trek?* The doctor could wave a portable wound-healer over your body and you would be cured instantly.

Researchers aren't promising an instant fix for breast cancer but they are investigating better methods to detect, control, and prevent the disease. Someday, probably in your lifetime, breast cancer will no longer be a life-threatening condition. Recent advances raise the hope that a prevention or cure will be possible. Look for exciting developments in these areas of research.

- Genetics—identifying genes which can increase the risk of breast cancer.
- Tumor growth factors—controlling the molecules that permit and encourage cancer growth.

- Drug development—improving existing treatments and developing new ones.
- Immunology—making the body's natural defense against cancer more effective.
- Chemoprevention—using drugs to lower the risk of breast cancer.

Will a test for the breast cancer gene become available?

Perhaps by the time you read this, a test to identify carriers of the mutant BRCA1 gene may be readily available. This mutant gene makes women susceptible to breast cancer. Women who carry a mutated form of BRCA1 face as much as an 80 percent chance of developing breast cancer by the time they are 65. They must also confront an increased chance of getting ovarian cancer. Women who do not carry the gene still face the same risk of breast cancer as women in the general population without a family history of it.

What are my options if I carry the mutated gene?

Two major options exist at the time of the writing of this book. Women who know they have the mutated gene can choose to live with the risk and carefully monitor their health. Or, they can opt for surgical removal of both breasts.

A double mastectomy greatly reduces the risk of breast cancer but does not eliminate it totally. Some breast tissue still remains behind after surgery and a very slight chance exists that breast cancer could arise in it.

Women who choose to keep their breasts need to perform monthly breast self-exams and see their nurse or doctor at least once every six months for a clinical breast exam. Monitoring by mammography or possibly by magnetic resonance imaging is also important. These measures cannot prevent breast cancer. But they usually catch cancer early enough that it can be easily treated. The drug tamoxifen is currently being studied to test its effectiveness in preventing breast cancer in high-risk women.

If you carry the mutated gene, seek out the most current advice available and go for counseling before you make a decision. New preventive treatments and better choices may be available.

Will screening techniques improve in the future?

New technologies already in existence may make it easier to spot breast-cancer tumors in the future. *Digitized mammograms* can record X-rays in computer code instead of making a picture on film. Special software can magnify tiny suspicious spots in the resulting computer image, making detection of very early cancer possible.

MRI scans can be customized to ignore cysts and fat, and to focus in on cancer. MRI technology may also revolutionize cancer surgery. A low-powered laser could be used to destroy cancer cells while an MRI scan continually shows the surgeon where to aim the laser.

The *PET scanner* is a high tech machine that provides images of the inside of the body. Like the CAT scanner and MRI, the PET scanner relies on computer technology.

The "PET" in PET-scan stands for *positron emission tomography*. A quick physics lesson may help you understand how it works:

Before undergoing a PET scan, a patient is injected with a solution of radioactive sugar. The sugar circulates throughout the body and is taken up by active cells. This special sugar gives off *positrons*—very tiny particles that are even smaller than atoms. When positrons meet electrons (the tiny particles surrounding the nucleus of an atom) they explode and give off radiation. The PET scanner detects and records the location of the radiation. Its computer translates this information into a picture. Since many tumor cells take up sugar faster than normal cells, the PET scan can disclose their location. It may be able to catch many of the breast cancers that mammograms miss.

How will research at the molecular level help?

Research at the molecular level holds great promise. Scientists are looking for a way to detect the first signs of abnormal change on the surface of breast cells. They hope to find cancer so early that the abnormal cells will have divided only a few times. A needle biopsy could easily be performed to get rid of the cells and cure the cancer.

If scientists learn exactly how a normal cell turns into a cancer cell, they may be able to reverse the process. They may be able to find a treatment that turns cancer cells back to normal or a treatment that blocks precancerous cells and prevents them from becoming a fully-developed cancer.

Can resistance to cancer drugs be reduced?

Scientists may find a way to combat drug resistance in cancer cells. They know that a resistant cell manages to "pump" anti-cancer drugs out of itself. They also have discovered a gene that helps to make cancer cells resistant to anti-cancer drugs. Now, the researchers are trying to find drugs that will block drug resistance. If they are successful, chemotherapy will become more effective.

What is immunotherapy?

Researchers hope that mobilizing the body's immune system will make a better weapon against breast cancer than chemotherapy and hormone treatments. You are probably familiar with how your immune system works. When harmful microbes sneak past the skin and enter body tissues, amoeba-like white blood cells seek out the microbes and gobble them up. Other white blood cells—*lymphocytes*—aid in the fight. They recognize the distinct chemicals on the surface of each kind of microbe and produce a specific antibody to attack it. After the antibodies destroy the microbe, some antibodies stay in the bloodstream for years or even life. These antibodies will rally in the defense of the body if the microbe invades again.

You probably wonder what this has to do with battling cancer. One kind of lymphocyte, a *T-cell*, identifies and attacks cancer cells before they have a chance to multiply. *NK cells*—short for natural killers—pitch in. T-cells and NK cells destroy abnormal cells without harming healthy ones! They patrol the body like soldiers on the lookout for enemy invaders. Routinely, they detect and remove abnormal cells. Unfortunately, cancer cells sometimes grow undetected or reproduce so fast the immune system cannot catch them all. Somehow the cells "cloak" their abnormality from T-cells and NK cells and slip by them. Some kinds of white blood cells may turn traitor. They actually protect tumor cells from the onslaught of T-cells and NK cells.

The challenge for scientists is to find a way to stimulate a patient's immune system to battle cancer. They are investigating three different vaccination strategies:

- a vaccine to prevent cancer.
- a vaccine to immunize women against their own tumors to keep the cancer from spreading, and
- a vaccine to strengthen the immune system so it can better fight cancer cells.

What are monoclonal antibodies?

Monoclonal antibodies are antibodies that have been altered in the laboratory. When injected into a patient, monoclonal antibodies can find and attach themselves to cancer cells. Unfortunately, they have proven unsuccessful so far in destroying tumors. Scientists hope to fuse them with anti-cancer drugs that can be released when the antibody locates a cancer cell. These "smart bombs" would target and kill cancer cells while leaving healthy cells alone. Monoclonal antibodies may also prove useful in locating tumors so they can be treated with radiation.

What does all of this mean for me?

Your generation will have a better chance of beating the odds against breast cancer than your mother's. Sometime in the next century, detection will be possible at the very beginning stages of cancer development. Drug treatments will become less harsh and more effective. Mastectomies and lumpectomies will probably become obsolete.

In the meantime, you still need to protect yourself against breast cancer. If you have read Chapter Four you know what preventive measures to take against the disease. You also know what to do to detect it early. Now it's up to you to take charge of your health. As you grow older, keep yourself informed about new advances in the fight against breast cancer. *The more you know, the greater your options will be.* Try not to let the worry about breast cancer rule your life. Some research looks so promising that by the time you are thirty or forty, treating breast cancer may be as easy as treating an ear infection!

Glossary

Antioxidants: Chemicals that protect against cancer.

Areola: A circle of darker skin that surrounds the nipple.

Arteries: Blood vessels that carry oxygen-rich blood away from the heart to the tissues.

Benign tumor: A tumor that is *not* cancerous and does *not* spread to other parts of the body.

Beta-carotene: A yellow pigment found in the cells of brightly-colored fruits and vegetables.

Biopsy: The surgical removal of tissue so it can be checked for abnormalities.

Bone marrow: The innermost part of bone where blood cells develop.

Bone scan: A diagnostic test to determine whether there is any sign of cancer spread to the bones.

BRCA1: A gene that appears to be responsible for most inherited breast cancers.

Breast reconstruction: Surgery to replace a missing breast.

Breast self-exam: An examination of the breasts performed by oneself.

BSE: Breast self-exam.

Cancer: A disorder of the cells resulting in uncontrolled cell reproduction. There are about 100 different kinds of human cancers.

Capillaries: The smallest blood vessels.

Carcinomas: Cancers that arise in epithelial cells.

CAT-scan: Computerized axial tomography. A device that combines X-rays and computer technology to make detailed pictures of the body's soft tissues and internal organs.

Cell: The smallest living part of the body that can exist by itself.

Cell division: A process in which a full-grown cell divides into two new ones.

Cell membrane: The outer boundary of a cell.

Chemotherapy: A treatment that uses powerful drugs to fight cancer cells in the body.

Chromosomes: The threadlike structures within a cell's nucleus that contain genes and direct all the cell's activities.

Clinical breast exam: An examination of the breasts performed by a nurse or physician.

Colostrum: Liquid filled with antibodies to help a baby fight infections. It is produced by the breasts after a baby is born.

Computerized axial tomography: CAT-scan.

Cysts: Fluid-filled lumps that are almost never cancerous.

Cytoplasm: The fluid that surrounds the nucleus of a cell.

DDT: A particular pesticide that has been banned.

Diagnosis: Identification of a disease.

Digitized mammogram: A mammogram that is recorded in computer code instead of on x-ray film.

Discharge: A fluid that is secreted or released from the body.

Ducts: Tubes in the milk gland that lead from the lobules to the nipple.

Endosulfan: A pesticide used widely on fruits and vegetables.

Epithelial cells: Cells that line the milk ducts and milk glands, and cover the inside and outside surfaces of organs.

Estrogen: A female hormone produced mainly in the ovaries.

Fallopian tube: A tube leading from an ovary to the uterus.

Fatty acids: A fatty-acid molecule is a chain of hydrogen, carbon, and oxygen atoms. Three fatty acid molecules make up part of every fat molecule.

Fiber: The undigestible carbohydrates found in plant foods.

Fibroadenoma: A smooth, round lump that is harmless.

Genes: The structures on chromosomes that determine genetic traits.

Heredity: The passing of traits from parents to offspring.

Hormones: A chemical messenger made in one part of the body and transported to other parts through the blood. Hormones help regulate body activities such as growth, development, and reproduction.

Hormone therapy: A drug treatment that cuts off cell access to estrogen.

Immunotherapy: Treatment to strengthen the immune system.

Infiltrating cancer: A cancer that has broken through the borders of surrounding tissue and invaded it.

Inherited traits: Traits passed from parent to child through the genes.

In situ **cancer:** Very early cancer that has not spread to surrounding tissues.

Invasive cancer: A cancer that has broken through the borders of surrounding tissue and invaded it.

Inverted nipples: Nipples that pucker inward.

IV: An abbreviation for *intravenous*. It refers to equipment that places medicine directly into the bloodstream. The IV consists of a tube attached to a plastic bag containing the medicine. The other end of the tube is placed directly in a vein and the medicine drips from the bag and tube into the body.

Lobules: The milk-producing part of the milk gland in the breast.

Localized cancer: An invasive cancer that has spread to surrounding tissue but not to distant tissues.

Lump: A bump beneath the skin that can be felt.

Lumpectomy: Removal of the cancerous lump along with the rim of normal tissues surrounding it. Through a separate incision, a few lymph nodes from under the arm are also removed.

Lymph: The clear, almost colorless part of blood that seeps into spaces between the body cells.

Lymph nodes: Glands in the lymph system that form part of the body's defense system against germs and other harmful substances.

Lymph vessels: Structures in the lymph system that carry lymph fluid. Lymph vessels have thin walls and valves, and are similar to veins.

Lymphocytes: A kind of white blood cell that fights infection by producing antibodies.

Magnetic Resonance Imaging (MRI): A technique that uses magnetism to produce an image of the interior of the body.

Malignancy: A cancerous tumor.

Malignant tumor: A cancerous tumor.

Mammogram: A low-dose X-ray that gives a clear, detailed picture of breast tissue.

Mastectomy: Surgical removal of a breast

Menarche: The first period.

Menopause: The time in a woman's life when periods end.

Menstruation: The monthly discharge of the blood-filled lining of the uterus.

Metastasize: To move to a distant part of the body through the bloodstream or lymph system.

Milk glands: Glands in the breast that can produce milk.

Modified radical mastectomy: The removal of the breast, the lining of the chest muscles, and all the underarm lymph nodes.

Monoclonal antibodies: Antibodies that have been altered in the laboratory.

MRI: Magnetic Resonance Imaging.

Mutate: To change.

Mutation: A change in one or more genes that results in a new trait.

Negative nodes: Lymph nodes that are free of cancer.

Nipple: The small tip of the breast.

NK cells: Short for "natural killers"—white blood cells that attack cancer cells.

Noninherited traits: Traits acquired by an individual that were not passed on through the genes.

Noninvasive cancer: Cancer at an early stage that has not invaded surrounding tissues.

Nucleus: 1. The control center of the cell that directs all the cell's activities. 2. The dense, central part of an atom.

Omega-3 fatty acids: Fatty acids that may protect against the development of breast cancer.

Oncologist: A doctor who specializes in cancer treatment.

Organ: A group of different kinds of tissue that join together to perform a specific function.

Ovary: Female reproductive organ that produces eggs.

Ovulation: The release of an egg during the menstrual cycle.

Period: The time of menstruation.

PET scanner: Positron emission tomography. A machine that relies on computer technology and emissions from positrons to provide images of the inside of the body.

PMS: Premenstrual syndrome. Physical and emotional changes due to hormonal changes which take place in the week preceding menstruation.

Positive nodes: Lymph nodes with cancer.

Positrons: Very tiny particles that are even smaller than atoms. When positrons meet electrons they explode and give off radiation.

Precancerous growth: Abnormal cells that don't have all the characteristics of a cancer cell.

Predisposition: A tendency or susceptibility.

Preventive surgery: The removal of the ovaries to eliminate the major source of female hormones in the body.

Primary tumor: The place where a cancer first develops.

Progesterone: A female hormone produced in the ovaries.

Prosthesis: An artificial breast that is worn externally.

Protocol: A plan of treatment.

Pubic hair: Hair that appears at puberty and surrounds the external genitals.

Radiation: The transfer of energy by electromagnetic waves; nuclear radiation results from radioactivity—the breakdown of atomic nuclei.

Radiation therapy: A treatment that uses high-powered, invisible rays to damage cancer cells and prevent them from reproducing.

Radical mastectomy: The removal of the entire breast, the chest muscles beneath the breast, and all the underarm lymph nodes.

Radioactive chemical: A chemical that gives off invisible radiation.

Receptors: Structures on the surface of a cell which control the entry of estrogen.

Regional involvement: A cancer that has just begun to spread to other nearby tissues such as the skin or lymph nodes close by.

Remission: When a cancer seems to disappear.

Resistant: Cancer cells that are no longer harmed by anti-cancer drugs which worked before.

Risk: Chance of getting breast cancer.

Saturated fats: Fats that are solid at room temperature.

Screening: The examination of healthy people for early signs of cancer.

Secondary tumor: A tumor that develops at a site distant from the original tumor.

Second opinion: A consultation with an additional doctor.

Segmental mastectomy: Removal of the section of the breast with the tumor, some skin above it, and the lining of the chest muscle below it. Some lymph nodes are removed in a separate incision.

Sexual intercourse: The act of putting the male penis inside the female vagina.

Simple mastectomy: Removal of the breast and the lining of the chest muscles.

Staging: A system used to describe how far a breast cancer has spread.

Statistics: Facts that are presented in a manner which provides numerical information about a subject.

Systemic treatment: A treatment that involves the whole body, such as chemotherapy or hormone therapy.

Tamoxifen: An anticancer drug that prevents breast-cancer cells from acquiring estrogen.

T-cells: White blood cells that identify and attack cancer cells.

Tissue: A group of cells that grow and work together.

Tumor: A group of cells that grows together and crowds out other cells.

Ultrasound: The use of high-frequency sound waves to make outlines of structures in the body.

Unsaturated fats: Fats that are liquid at room temperature.

Uterus: The female reproductive organ which holds and nourishes a developing baby until birth.

Vaccine: A substance used to protect a person against a disease.

Veins: Blood vessels that return blood to the heart.

Visualization: A technique used to form a mental image.

Wartlike growths: Benign growths that can appear in the milk ducts near the nipple.

Weaning: Causing a baby to gradually become accustomed to food other than its mother's milk.

Further Reading

For information on handling sexual harassment, read *Safe, Strong, & Streetwise: Sexual Safety at Home, On the Street, On the Job, At Parties, & More* by Helen Benedict (Boston: Little Brown, 1987).

You can also purchase the booklet, "Tune In to Your Rights: A Guide for Teenagers about Turning Off Sexual Harassment." Send a $3.00 check or money order to:

> Programs for Educational Opportunity
> 1005 School of Education Building
> University of Michigan
> Ann Arbor, MI 48109-1259

To obtain more detailed information about the Food Guide Pyramid, you can order *The Food Guide Pyramid*

Brochure from the U.S. Government. Send a check or money order for $1.00, made out to "Superintendent of Documents" to:

> Consumer Information Center
> Item 159
> Pueblo, CO 81009

You may find these books helpful in changing your eating habits:

> *Eat Well* by Miriam Moss (New York: Crestwood House, 1993)
>
> *Fats* by Dr. Alvin Silverstein, Virginia Silverstein, and Robert Silverstein (Brookfield, CT: Millbrook Press, 1992)
>
> *Nutrition: What's in the Food We Eat?* by Dorothy Patent (New York: Holiday House, 1992)
>
> *Good for Me! All About Food in 32 Bites* by Marilyn Burns (Boston: Little Brown, 1978)

Some good books that may help you deal with your mother's breast cancer are:

> *Moms Don't Get Sick* by Pat Brack with Ben Brack (Aberdeen, SD: Melius Publishing, Inc., 1990)
>
> *Afraid to Ask* by Judylaine Fine (New York: Beech Tree Books, 1986)
>
> *The Long Way Home* by Barbara Cohen (New York: Lothrop, Lee & Shepard, 1990)

When a Parent Is Very Sick by Eda LeShan (Boston: Little Brown, 1986)

These books may help you understand the process of grieving. They may be available in your library:

How It Feels When a Parent Dies by Jill Krementz (New York: Alfred A. Knopf, 1981)

Loss and How to Cope with It by Joanne E. Bernstein (New York: Seabury Press, 1977)

Learning to Say Good-bye When a Parent Dies by Eda LeShan (New York: Macmillan, 1976)

When Bad Things Happen to Good People by Rabbi Harold S. Kushner (New York: Avon, 1982)

Photo Credits

page 31: La Leche League International

pages 37, 102, and 103: Photo Researchers, Inc.

pages 38 and 39: Custom Medical Stock Photo

page 77: National Fisheries Institute, Inc.

page 80: United Fresh Fruit & Vegetable Association

page 82: U.S. Department of Agriculture/U.S. Department
of Health and Human Services

pages 87, 94, and 96: American Cancer Society

page 95: Kathy Sloane/Photo Researchers, Inc.

pages 104, 117, and 119: Custom Medical Stock Photo

page 105: Courtesy of Hitachi North America

page 112: Courtesy of Philips Medical Systems
North America

Index

186 🦋 WILL I GET BREAST CANCER?

Carole Garbuny Vogel

writes nonfiction books for young readers. Some of her books include *Why Mount St. Helens Blew Its Top*, *The Great Midwest Flood of 1993*, *Humphrey, the Wrong-Way Whale*, and *The Great Yellowstone Fire*, the last of which was named an NSTA-CBC Outstanding Science Trade Book for Children in 1990. In 1994, the Society of Children's Book Writers and Illustrators awarded a work-in-progress grant to Ms. Vogel.

In addition to her book-writing, Ms. Vogel has contributed articles to encyclopedias and science textbooks. Her essays have appeared in several magazines, including *Ladies' Home Journal*, *Good Housekeeping*, and *Working Mother*.

Carole G. Vogel graduated from Kenyon College with a B.A. in biology and received an M.A.T. in elementary education from the University of Pittsburgh. She taught for five years before becoming a science editor and running her own educational consulting business. She lives in Lexington, Massachusetts with her husband and their two teenagers.